Beat the Markets!

A Retail Trader's Journey to Success through a Maze of Misinformation, Opportunists & False Promises.

by
Chris Wilson

Published by: Automated Online Trading
www.automatedonlinetrading.com

Printed in Australia
First Printing, 2015
Copyright © 2015 Chris Wilson

ISBN: 978-0-9943940-0-2

ISBN 978-0-9943940-0-2

9 780994 394002 >

To James & Phyllis, and Mooky - Lifelong Thanks......
for Everything.

To Nicole and James

Disclaimer

Attention Australian Residents:

The information contained in this text is for information purposes only. I do not hold an Australian Financial Services (AFS) license, and as such, the information herein is not intended to be a financial product or investment advice or a recommendation. I do not endorse any particular investment and you should seek independent advice from a financial advisor who holds an AFS license before making any investment decision.

This information herein has been prepared without taking into account the objectives, financial situation or needs of any individual. Before making an investment decision, prospective investors should consider the appropriateness of the information having regard to their own objectives, financial situation and needs and seek legal and taxation advice appropriate to their jurisdiction.

Past performance Past performance information given in this text is given for illustrative purposes only and should not be relied upon and is not an indication of future performance.

Future performance Forward-looking statements, opinions and estimates provided in this text are based on assumptions and contingencies which are subject to change without notice, as are statements about market and industry trends, which are based on interpretations of current market conditions.

Forward-looking statements including projections, guidance on future earnings and estimates are provided as a general guide only and should not be relied upon as an indication or guarantee of future performance. Actual results, performance or achievements may vary materially for many projections because events and actual circumstances frequently do not occur as forecast and these differences can be material.

Please also see Appendix I – The Usual Disclaimers for further discussion on the importance of understanding disclaimers.

Contents

Figures

Tables

Beat the Markets!

A Retail Trader's Journey to Success through a Maze of Misinformation, Opportunists & False Promises.

by

Chris Wilson

Introduction

What Inspired this Book?

Over ten years of self-inflicted 'pain' are behind writing this book. The pain has come from learning about trading the hard way. It is said there is no substitute for experience. I wish there were.

I had been trading in shares, futures and commodities – in a way that many other people have – losing money through a combination of over expectation, lack of knowledge and acting on the so-called expertise of 'professional' advisors or instructors. However, as this book testifies, I have survived it all ... and I am now passing on my lessons learned, so that you and many others may benefit.

My interest in trading started in the summer of 1977. I had just graduated from high school and was about to begin a tour of duty in the United States Air Force. A book on stock trading caught my eye in a local store while on a road trip with my family from California to the East Coast. Like all teenagers (and most adults) I had dreams of riches from Wall Street. Although I read the book from cover to cover and became entirely absorbed in it, life got very busy, and my interest in trading took a back seat for many years.

Since then my life has followed a clear pathway of intensive development contributing towards an understanding of the field by applying my leading-edge professional training and experience to effectively analyse the topic of trading.

Looking at my background early on, I left the US Air Force as a decorated veteran who had been focusing on intelligence data collection, data handling system analysis and design and signals intelligence analysis. There is probably no better place in the world to learn and practice multi-level analysis than the USAF.

Using this expertise, I then spent 18 years in the US aerospace and defense industry with Martin Marietta Astronautics specializing in satellite and IT systems development. This included real-time operations as a satellite vehicle technical advisor in the vehicle flight software, command and data handling systems, and attitude control systems areas.

I supported NASA Shuttle mission planning, integration and operations for the NASA Atlantis STS-27 shuttle mission. This mission was extremely intensive in its planning and execution. Being only the second mission after the Challenger space shuttle disaster, the entire team carried massive responsibility.

After moving to Australia in 2000, I spent the next 13 years in the ICT industry with Cisco Systems as a senior manager specializing in technology projects and program management, while holding key leadership roles across the Asia-Pacific region.

Throughout much of my period in Australia I have been trading stock options. (My experience included one year as an instructor trainee with a popular options trading education provider. In the light of what you will read in this book, please excuse me not naming that company.) Like so many other people, starting my trading journey, I took many courses and read many books. I soon began to recognise that 99% of them were misleading, deceptive or incomplete.

My short but certainly not sweet experience (although I did enjoy the student interaction) as an options trading instructor confirmed this from a 'behind the curtain' perspective.

I discovered automated trading systems around 2009, purchasing my first one for futures markets. This system, and subsequent systems I acquired, mirrored my experiences with almost every book and course on trading: reality did not meet with the expectations set by the author, developer, or instructor.

Therefore, using my analytical training and experience, I set out to develop a robust system and the development methodology to maximise my probability of success. That process and the systems that I refer to in this book are the culmination of some six years of intensive research, development and testing ... and they work.

Today, I not only build my systems using that methodology, I also actively and successfully trade the systems live.

I don't know anyone else who can claim as intensive a personal history when it comes to systems and analysis ... plus the practical experience of having put much of my own money 'on the line' to continually test and improve my automated trading systems. My story and insights are revealed here publicly for the first time.

This book is meant for those just starting to look at trading, or the struggling trader with some experience. In either case, please note that some of the concepts in the book will be new to you and you may have to read them more than once to gain understanding and absorb all the value that I know this book will bring to you.

Chris Wilson

August 2015

Chapter 1

The Industry and Me

It was some time before I recognised that the desire for trading success and profits by retail (home-based) traders generates an large industry fraught with peril. As I've already alluded to, most of the so-called education and trading systems providers, along with many of the books on the subject are close to worthless.

The vast majority of them paints an inaccurate picture of the reality of trading. Mostly they provide a mass of misinformation and may charge a small fortune for methodologies that do nothing more than allow you to lose money.

Award winning trader and author Kevin Davey writes:

"In general, any performance information you receive from someone wanting to sell you signals, a black box system, a subscription, trading room, and so on should not be trusted. An excellent general rule is: don't believe any of it." (Davey, 2014)

He also states that his approach is extreme. Maybe. But I agree, as do many other traders I know that echo the same sentiment.

My Stages of Development

Many traders have gone through similar phases of development in their trading experiences. You may quickly relate to each of them, depending on where you are in your trading journey. The phases are not discrete, and you will notice some overlap between them.

The Discretionary Phase

Like many traders, I started out as a discretionary trader. At that time, the Internet was still relatively new, and not everyone had a home computer. Mainstream brokers were now accessible via the Internet and costs were becoming affordable. So, I established an E*TRADE account and gave it a shot.

How exciting! My approach was simple. I bought stocks in companies that produced products that I used and respected, like Photoshop. My first trade was Adobe stock – purchased at about $60, and I rode it to $120 per share. Wow! I had doubled my money in a very short time. What a trading genius I was!

I also dabbled in telecom stocks just buying what was going up. I had no real idea what I was doing and made money – as happens to many beginning traders. Of course, I made money. Any idiot could have, and would have, under the then-current circumstances, the dot.com bubble bull market.

Early in March 2000, after moving to Australia and about to get married; I pulled out of my trading accounts. Later that year, the dot.com bubble began to burst. Stocks started to move sideways and sank, companies folded, and fortunes were lost. By sheer luck, I missed the crash and came away unscathed.

Many traders start out the way I did. Just buying stock in a company that they believe in, some intuition they may have had, perhaps getting a hot tip from a friend or a financial paper, or some 'market expert' on TV. If they happen to make money, as I did, they tell well-embellished trading stories of their great success.

The Technical Phase

Settling into my new life in Australia, it was about six years before my interest in markets resurfaced. Like so many would-be traders, I had the dream of trading for a living and giving up my high-stress corporate lifestyle. So I started to read trading books and set aside some funds to sign up for courses with what I'll refer to as Trading Education Providers (TEP).

I was on my way to real trading success! Or so I thought.

From the books I was reading, I started to learn about technical analysis and started moving from my seat-of-the-pants discretionary phase to my technical phase. I was learning how to read charts, draw trend lines, look for patterns and use indicators that would help me (supposedly) predict where the market may go next.

An advertisement about being able to 'rent stocks' and 'buy insurance for your trades', sparked my curiosity. It referred to trading stock options ('renting shares') and so, I added options to my list of things to learn.

After going to a couple of free seminars, I signed up with a popular options TEP. The first course was a set of books and accompanying CDs that covered many different types of options trades, along with a two-day course that you could re-attend for perpetuity. I thought, "Great! I can keep going back until I get it!" It seemed like a good deal so, very much enthused, I started to go through all of the course material and attended my first live course.

Along with the options specific topics and technical analysis subjects being taught in class, a long list of additional courses and software packages were presented. The instructors all appeared to be knowledgeable, and all informed the class that they traded for a living. That was fantastic since I had similar goals.

Technical analysis and options were not the simplest topics. However, I figured with my technology education and a sound background in the aerospace and IT industries, I shouldn't have any issues understanding and absorbing the material and becoming a trading success in no time.

My options TEP offered charting and options analysis software to help find and analyse trading opportunities, which included Elliot Wave analysis, along with all of the other usual charting package features - tonnes of indicators, drawing tools and the like.

However, being a software professional, I soon became very unimpressed with the usability of the software and wrote to the CEO of the options TEP company documenting the data, capabilities and ease-of-use issues I had found with the software.

"While the options TEP software package has some excellent features, I have found that it does not meet my expectation for overall quality and capability considering its price point," I wrote.

In retrospect, I meant, *especially* considering its price point. It cost thousands of dollars; quite a lot more than the professional charting and analysis program that I use today, and far less capable. However, being committed to becoming a successful trader and also believing then that I would be making big money, I "invested' in the software. Surely it had to be worth the money. Live and learn.

Unknown to me at the time, I was on my way to a state known as 'indicator fascination', in which I would suffer from for a considerable period.

The options TEP software got me started, and my indicator fascination did not end until about two years later. I was in search of the Holy Grail - which the Monty Python team also failed to find. The charting package plotted Elliot Wave legs and labelled them, it had Fibonacci...everything and much, much more. Further, any indicator that wasn't in the basic package could be purchased from the friendly options TEP as an add-on.

The System Trading Phase

This phase started initially using a somewhat rudimentary built-in back-testing engine that was part of the options TEP software package I had bought. The engine enabled me to define trade entry and exit criteria and test them against historical daily data, resulting in a basic performance summary for analysis. Of course, the options TEP offered an add-on package of 10 systems to test and apply to live trading to "... Show you how to consistently build winning systems". Like most of their add-on packages and courses, it cost a couple of thousand dollars – and I went for it. (DOH!)

At this point, let me make it clear that while I may sound off about many of the purchasing decisions I made along my trading journey - some of which were of dubious value and took advantage of an unknowing customer's (me) ignorance - everything I bought furthered my progress and enhanced my advancement up the learning curve to arrive at the level I am at now. So, in one way or another, they contributed varying levels of value. I was now learning more about trading systems and also had a small selection of systems to test and to trade.

The systems and trading methods, generating directional or trend trades, did not get the results as advertised. Of course, now looking back at the add-on systems, I can see why I did not achieve the success that they promised.

I started to focus more on non-directional stock options trades ... Iron Condors, Calendars, Double Calendars, Diagonals. You name it, and I traded it.

I was taking classes, reading books, learning and trading in every spare minute, while holding down a very demanding Fortune 500 job that had me in the air throughout Asia most of the time. In brief, I now needed to take a break and also wanted time to progress further on non-directional options trading.

During this break, I also worked part-time as an instructor for the same options TEP outfit where I began my options trading – travelling around Australia and New Zealand teaching the same two-day course in which I was once a student. Now, 'behind the curtain', I was able to see how the instructors operated ... and was less than impressed.

Their methods were predatory. Each session was structured to teach you just enough, and tug on your emotions so that you would lay down the money for more classes, software, etc. It was typical to end a two-day session with a recommended trade, a product of their Elliot Wave analysis software. Potentially, you could easily make a few thousand dollars very quickly, which would more than cover any purchases you would make that day.

To the inexperienced trader, this is very tempting and is a great sales tactic. Except that it is just that, a tactic, and it is dishonest. I met students that had invested in these 'recommendations' and had lost thousands of dollars.

Most of the instructors at the options TEP proclaimed to their classes that they traded for a living. But, in reality they TRAINED for a living, and some of them didn't trade at all.

After six months into my contract, I had seen enough and decided to become inactive. Although grateful for the experience, I was not comfortable with the company or the role and felt my time would be better spent researching systems and options trading.

Still suffering from indicator fascination, I bought a set of CDs with custom indicators and training videos and joined the live chat room of a popular futures day-trader in the US. This trader used indicators I had not seen before, and he was sponsored by one of my brokers in a webinar. Surely they HAD to be good, and he HAD to know what he was doing. However, his ability and his knowledge were debatable. I did learn about futures and about day-trading to a certain degree but was not impressed with the live trading room, nor with the instructors live trading results.

It came to mind during one the trading room sessions that there had to be a way to automate my trading and reduce the effects of the human factors that work against you in trading - fatigue, sickness and the fact a person can only just do a handful of things at once.

Up to that point, I had not realized that a trader at home could automate entries and exits. This concept opened new doors for me, recognising that the greatest advantage could be gained by automating direction trades in the futures markets.

The Automated System Trading Phase

Obsessed with the concept trading. After all I couldn't automate them and, by this point, I was getting more uncomfortable with managing options trades in the US market because of the time difference.

After undertaking some research, I purchased my first system development platform, AmiBroker. A well featured, flexible platform, it also had automated trading capability with my then current broker, Interactive Brokers. Best of all, it was very inexpensive, only a few hundred dollars at the time.

Finally, with a capable, reliable, charting indicator and system development platform, I was on my way to tackling system trading.

The first action was to duplicate the indicators I had learned about from my futures day-trader. It was a time-consuming process, but I was able to re-code them in AmiBroker's Formula Language (AFL). It wasn't hard, having been an old Cobol, C++, Java programmer earlier in my career.

During this phase, I began to see indicators in their true light as a valuable tool to make money ... for the organization selling them. I could now create systems and trade histories based on the indicators and determine their statistical effectiveness *before I traded using them,* and not just take the claims of the seller as true.

I took to trading methods that my books and classes offered, automated the entries and exits, optimized the input parameters and tested the systems using historical data. However, many just did not work. Others simply did not lend themselves to automation.

I saw some impressive results in my historical back-testing, but this was the infant stage of my automated system development. At the time, I did not understand the impact of over-optimization and did not have a robust method of developing and testing systems.

My vision was to trade multiple systems at the same time, perhaps with different brokers from the same platform, which my current platform, AmiBroker could not do. Research led me to choose MultiCharts, an award winning trading platform (compatible with TradeStation, an industry leader in trading automation). I trade with MultiCharts today.

Armed with the desire to find success with automated trading as soon as possible, I undertook some research online and then purchased a membership with an experienced Certified

Technical Advisor (CTA) who offered a suite of automated day and swing trading systems. These were TradeStation and MultiCharts compatible, and I bought the open code versions so that I could understand exactly what was behind each of them.

Any given night, I'd have 3-5 systems actively trading in the US markets while I slept. I saw limited success, but not the consistent results that I craved.

My corporate break now over, I would spend any spare time learning as much as possible about trading systems development and testing methods. I stopped trading my purchased systems live and set out to define my own system development methodology - one that would optimize the probabilities of a robust, reliable automated trading system.

After more than a year of testing, analysis, testing and more analysis (and some mentoring from an experienced, full time retail automated trader with extremely high integrity) I completed the process. Very importantly, I now fully understood why the 'professionally-developed' systems I had bought had not worked as advertised.

Today, with an end-to-end fully-tested automated trading system development and qualification process, I trade daily (or nightly), while I research, develop new, and continually improve my systems.

In writing this book, I hope to help others avoid the very expensive, time-consuming and highly frustrating learning and development curve.

More on the Industry

Education/System Providers

Do a quick search on Google and you'll find scores of education providers, offering a series of learning sessions over the Internet or in-class. Just yesterday a friend pointed out a 'trading academy' that was offering an introductory course for just under US$700. Consisting of ten one-hour modules, it claims:

"Over the course of (10 one-hour modules spanning) four weeks, students of all levels, just like you, learn to trade with confidence by focusing on both the technical and fundamental aspects of trading with our help and support throughout, providing you with a solid understanding of what is required in order to successfully trade stocks, currency and commodity markets."

Really? In four weeks, you'll be able to successfully trade stocks, currencies *and* commodity markets? It states that they "will provide you with a solid understanding", which is dubious claim in itself, but the implication is that you will be able to trade successfully over all three of these primary asset classes.

Now, it won't take long to discover that this won't happen in four weeks. Fortunately the 'training academy' has come to the same conclusion, because it immediately offers you a follow-on course. This one will teach you how to become a successful professional trader ... for another $1,400.

Great!   But don't believe it.

Does it make sense that this company (sorry, 'academy') is going to teach you a skill that enables you to become as a professional trader earning tens of thousands of dollars each year, for the rest of your working life, all for just over $2,000?

How likely is that really going to be? If it were so cheap and easy to do, why don't you know more people doing it? My guess is you don't know even one.

The site boasts more than 120,000 graduates, and each course has 5-star ratings based on almost 300 reviews, the exact same number of reviews on each course. Might you be suspicious?

There is no mention of actual live trading histories or the track records of successful graduates. Nor do they supply any performance history - live or simulated - for the trading strategies they offer.

You've got the picture, so I won't spend any more time picking such sites apart. There are dozens like this throughout the world. I just hope that, after reading this book, you will recognise all of them for what they are.

Automated Systems Vendors

Automated System Vendors offer software to run on one the many automated trading platforms. (Such as NinjaTrader, MultiCharts, TradeStation and others.)

The prices of these systems can run from hundreds to many thousands of dollars and, like most things related to trading, there are no guarantees (other than you will experience losses).

Firstly, merely purchasing a system, installing it and running it will not lead to great riches. Typically, potential purchasers are unaware of the complexities of systems development. Vendors take advantage of this lack of knowledge with fantastic equity curve charts, performance statistics and quite unreasonable claims. Being successful with an automated system is not as easy as these vendors make it sound.

There are many aspects. You:
- must first qualify the system
- need to determine if the system profile matches your personality and expectations
- need to know how to assess the system's performance based on the performance report contents.

This knowledge is provided in the 'Assessing a trading system' chapters 8-11 of this book.

Brokers

Brokers are a necessary part of trading. Some are good, some are not so good. Most of them survive on the constant cycle of traders entering the markets, and they know that most of them will only be able to trade for a short time.

Therefore, they market to unknowing potential customers - offering low commissions and margins and touting their built-in charts, indicators and tools that they claim will help you to find 'winning trades'.

Adopt a "prove it" attitude when are considering any trading-related offering. Don't take the advertised claims at face value.

Let's Move On

For now, that's a high enough dose of the realities of the industry. You are looking for advice that will take you into the direction you want to go, but avoiding the pitfalls. You'll get more as you read onward and realize that perhaps it is the misunderstood nature of markets themselves that drive the industry to be as it is. Also, be sure that although few, there are reputable and knowledgeable resources out there for the aspiring trader.

My journey to becoming a consistent, successful retail trader included buying and reading many books on trading subjects, joining numerous courses run by TEPs and also working as an instructor for a TEP. All of this gave me valuable insights into the investment industries – and where they fall down.

Most traders will not experience the level of success that promoters have promised, and they give up. If I had known what

I know today, my trading experience would have been significantly easier and my learning curve shorter. I discovered that I am not alone. What I have experienced is commonplace among traders – but they don't talk about it much outside their own circles.

In this book, you will be able to recognise the factors that have led to your disappointment with trading or, if new, avoid them altogether. I have been along the same path but, having had unique opportunities to learn valuable lessons; I have also experienced the joy of breaking through from failure to success.

Among other proven concepts, I will introduce you to automated trading systems. Many people are not aware that you can run a fully automated trading system from your computer at home, and that a large selection of brokers support automated trading platforms. There will be more on this later in the book.

So, now that we have looked at some of the realities of the trading industry through the lens of my experience, let's get into the more realistic and practical aspects of trading.

Resource: If you would like a list of trusted resources visit www.automatedonlinetrading.com where you will find a list of excellent books, information sources and training providers that I trust.

Things to Remember

- Providing education is an industry. Many providers simply want to make money and take great advantage of 'wanna-be' traders.

- Watch out for 'indicator fascination'. It is a phase that most traders experience - but there is no holy grail.

- Adopt a "prove it" attitude when are considering any trading related offering. Don't take the advertised claims at face value,

- Never purchase a trading approach, indicator, system without historical proof of performance (more on this throughout this book).

- Scrutinize guarantees and be fully aware of their terms in the fine print. The longer the guarantee, the better.

Chapter 2

Let's Be Realistic

High expectations

When I decided to pursue trading seriously, I had the same aspirations as many other people ... dreams of learning how to make great money and learning it quickly. And, like most others, I had set my expectations way too high.

Although not expecting to rival billionaire trader Warren Buffett, I certainly thought that if only I could just emulate a small percentage of the success enjoyed by the legendary Larry Williams, I'd be doing great. Larry was already a successful futures trader before hitting the headlines by winning the '1987 World Cup of Futures Trading', turning 10,000 dollars into 1.1 million dollars in 12 months using real money.

However, Larry's daughter – the Academy Award-winning actor Michelle Williams – was no slouch either. She learned trading by watching her father. Ten years after Larry's historic achievement, she blew away the competition to win the '1997 World Cup of Futures Trading' with a 900% return on her starting money – demonstrating the benefits of having unlimited free access to an excellent mentor with a proven track record.

I was heavily influenced by the dozens of advertisements and websites that showed how easy it would be to make a fortune just by using somebody's 'XYZ' trading system. Unlike Larry, who actually can and does trade successfully, most of these guys were indeed making fortunes - mainly by selling their systems to people like me.

In 2005, when I decided to pursue trading even more seriously, I was an IT professional with a successful career and earning well over $100,000 per year. That was a lot of income in those days. It took a while for me to realize what it would literally take, and how tough it would be, to replace my salary with trading income.

For example, the best money managers with all the resources in the world are regarded as absolute stars if they make 30% or more per year for their clients. So, I would need $300,000 in my trading account and earn from it at least 30% each year, just to make near $100,000. Realistically, I had only $100,000 set available for trading. So even if I happened to match a good money manager performance, it would only result in about $30,000 per year…in theory.

As a side note, realize that it is possible for the lone retail trader to beat the 30% profits per year – not easy, but it is possible.

The books written by industry figure Jack Schwager - for example, his *Market Wizards* series - profile many successful professional traders. So, it's not hard to find verified, factual examples of people who have been winning consistently over extended periods of time. It is a fact.

However, it is important to balance his conclusions with the widely accepted, popularly quoted, yet daunting statistic that

More than 90% of self-directed or retail traders lose money.

So, there is a broad gap between the professionals and the punters, who comprise the vast majority of people who trade financial instruments across the world.

Many studies support the fact most small and inexperienced traders lose money. This is due to a variety of factors that are being addressed in this book.

However, don't be disheartened. This information is presented to open your eyes to reality. It is certainly possible to make a million dollars a year from trading or to become a billionaire trader. However, the average operator will almost certainly not achieve this.

This book is specially designed to increase the odds in your favour significantly - and the techniques and concepts you will learn are exactly the ones that I apply personally.

So, how do you take control of your investing; reducing risks and improving the opportunities to make consistent profits trading the markets?

We will explore the factors that contribute to failure and also explore how to combat them using that newfound knowledge to increase your probabilities of making profitable trades throughout the year.

What 'others' won't tell you

Two components of successful trading are
* having a reasonable expectation of *dollars* and
* applying some common *sense*.

You don't have to necessarily lower your expectations, perhaps just expand your timescale.

We have already said that you can't just buy a system from a vendor and start shouting, *"Wow! Look at how my bank balance is zooming. No wonder my bank manager wants to take me out to dinner, again."*

While it is certainly possible to make significant money trading, do not expect this to happen overnight.

Before you can build a high brick wall, you need to put down sound foundations or the structure will collapse. Now, imagine that the wall consists of $1000 bricks.

The foundation for your wall is
- Education,
- Experience and
- Expertise

Get these three 'E's right and you will then be on your way. That is where I am about to take you. They will help to de-risk the journey you are about to take. Let's start with what I call the 'Dollars & Sense' of trading.

Dollars

Rather than aiming to make millions in profits over a year, let's set a conservative, realistic goal of $7000-10,000 per year. One can do more, one can certainly do less, but this is a reasonable target when looking at a system trading, in this case, a single contract at a time in the futures market. (More on futures and contracts in chapter 7.)

Sense

Q: How long does it take before you can learn and experience enough to become a proficient trader and see the positive cash flow reflected in consistently rising bank balances?

A: Perhaps three to five years ... and that is if you are doing very well.

Like many beginning traders I had runs of profits, and would feel competent and happy. Then runs of losses inevitably quickly killed the confidence and elation. It had taken several years before I was just breaking even. Despite all of the books I had read and the courses I had taken, I didn't understand why my trading was not successful.

Often, it takes traders longer to be successful (if they achieve success at all). They may make money early on along the way, but this is typically due to chance …and does not continue.

I started with stock options (and enjoy trading them today.) But I also wanted to learn about futures and 'fell in love' with them. Also, I had started doing long term manual trades, progressed to day-trading, and finally settled on a swing-trading automated approach. Once I focused on those particular paths, it took even more time and effort to get to the point where I am now. So, it may also take you some time to sort out what works for you in trading.

Your long-term success will depend on your commitment, trading method and your skills. If you are just starting to trade, you need to realize that it may take several years before you are consistently making money. Therefore, you must be committed to the journey, as it will not be an easy road.

Trading is a craft that takes years to master. That's right, years. For example, reading a book on becoming a maker of fine furniture won't automatically lift you into the highest echelons of that industry.

You need the three 'E's:

- Education. The key is here is quality. You have made a start by reading this, and as a trader there will always be something new to learn about markets, systems, etc.
- Experience. Gained over time, you will trade, and you will make errors. Learning from those errors will make you more proficient, which means more profits.

- Expertise. The end result of education and experience, it is the end goal that takes years to achieve.

You can minimize those errors, shorten your learning curve, and build that expertise sooner by following someone who has been on the same path you wish to follow; and you'll understand how by the end of this book.

And, just so you know, like many, I came into the game excited about trading and perhaps looking for excitement from trading. While I gain great satisfaction and thoroughly enjoy trading markets, my day-to-day routine is not exciting, and I don't want it to be.

In fact, the best trading is boring (i.e. sensible) ... and that is the way it should be unless you are not interested in making money. Excitement is not a good thing when trading.

Time for some examples

By now, hopefully, any unrealistic expectations you may have had have been pushed aside. So, let's start by referring to the trading system mentioned earlier, again, with its goal of making from $7000-10,000 per year from trading one contract in the futures market.

If you are not familiar with equity curve graphs, they are simply a visual representation of the profits and losses generated by the trades in a trading system over a timespan or series of trades.

Here is an excellent example of a trading system's equity curve. Credit for the strong performance is due to the trading system that it is based on, which I trade personally.

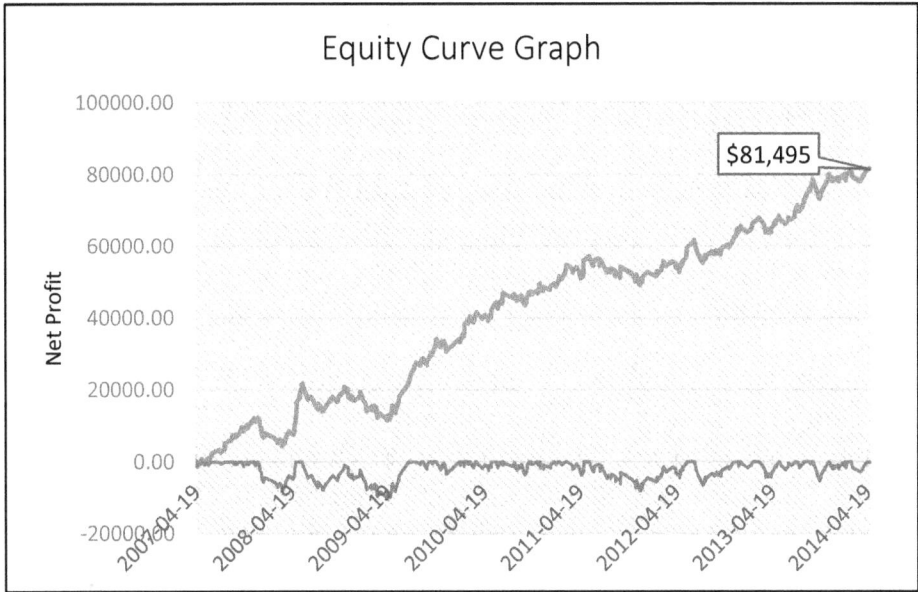

Figure 1 - Trading System Equity Curve Graph

This graph illustrates an example of a trading system that has been developed and qualified applying a methodology that results in robust, reliable trading systems (more in upcoming chapters). It's a pretty good system, as it continues at a roughly 45-degree angle with low drawdown periods.

Plotted in red is the drawdown amount at any given point in the equity curve. The drawdown is represented by those points in the equity curve that move from a high point to a lower point, or when the system is losing money from the most recent high in profits. Draw DOWN is an important aspect of any trading system and, to be successful; you will have to get used to it. Period.

There is no way to avoid it and is part of the cost of 'doing business', as it were. Therefore, it is closely linked to the opportunity.

Some terms you need to understand

Position sizing and diversification are two key concepts that you will need to understand to be a successful trader.

Position sizing is a powerful tool that traders use to maximize their profits from a trading system. Although it is a very complex subject involving many factors, with thick, math-laden books dedicated to it, it can be explained simply.

Position sizing defines what formula you will apply to your trading system to determine when to increase its trade size. For example, in a futures trading system (like our example above, which is based on one contract), applying a position sizing method would determine when the trade size would be increased from a single contract to two contracts, from two to three and so on.

In Figure 2 below is an equity curve graph of the same example system shown in Figure 1 (which is based on a single contract), now with an algorithm known as *fixed-risk position sizing* applied to it. With fixed-risk position sizing a specified percentage of total account equity is risked on each trade. As equity increases the system increases/decreases the number of contracts used in the system based on that formula.

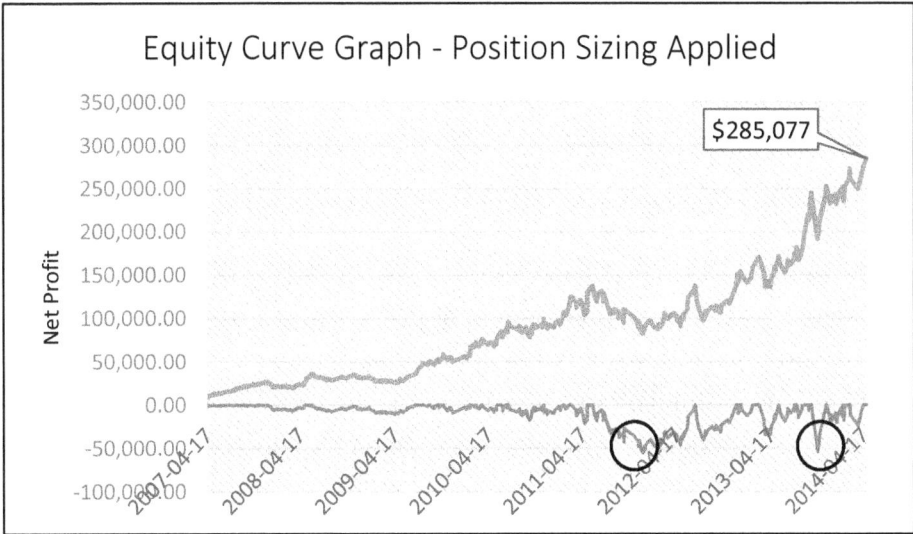

Figure 2 - Equity Curve Graph with Position Sizing

Compare the profit in Figure 1 with Figure 2. With such results, it would be almost criminal only to trade the system with one single contract, versus applying position sizing and maximizing the profit available using the system.

The effect on the long-term profits of the system is apparent. Also obvious but overlooked by many is the drawdown. There's that word again. Get used to it. It has been the reason for the failure of many a would-be trader. Look at the above chart: would you be able to endure the drawdown of $50,000 noted by the circles on the graph? (The answer: Yes, if you have confidence in your trading system.)

Diversification is another trading topic that can be very complex and it can be applied to investments in many different ways. Like position sizing, there are entire books dedicated to the subject, but it can be explained simply in the context of system trading.

Uncertainty is a fact of trading which you will have to get used to; realizing that,
even with a system that has been statistically vetted and robustly tested, there is no guarantee of what will occur in the future. You have no idea just when those drawdown periods may occur versus the times when you may experience a run of profits.

Let's say you are trading the example system and you want to trade an additional system, as there is that chance it may not make money, and you want to increase your chances to make profits. Wouldn't it be great to have an additional system that tended to act differently at different times than the original system?

Of course it would! Let's say the second system is typically in a run of profits when the first system is in a drawdown period based on historical data analysis. This being the case the systems would be referred to as being 'uncorrelated' while two systems whose profits rise and fall at the same time are correlated.

There are levels of correlation, and they vary based on the length of time being analysed. In Figure 3 there are two systems equity graphs plotted. While there are time spans that the two are somewhat correlated there are also time spans that are not.

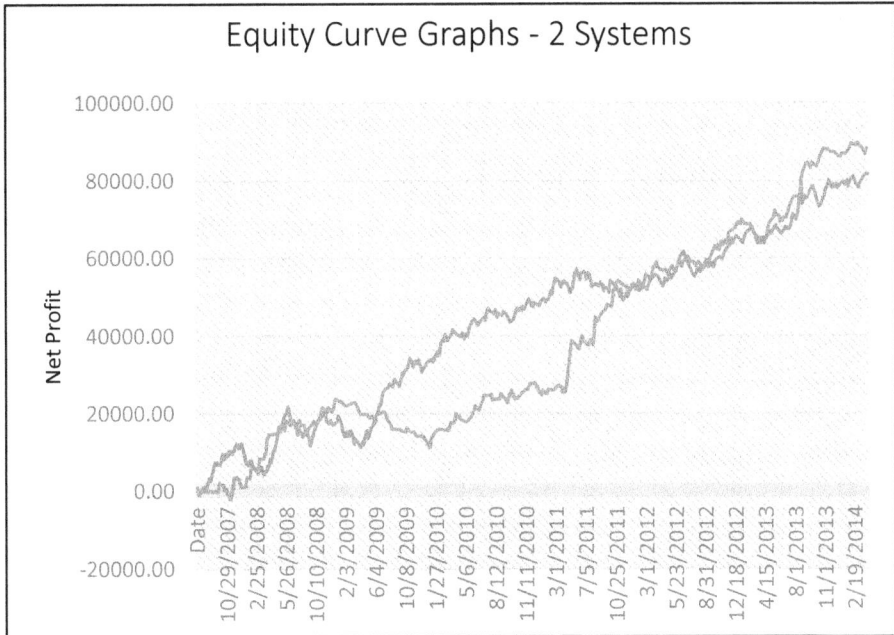

Figure 3 - Equity Curve Graphs - 2 Systems

The ability to make additional profits from an additional system, offset drawdown periods in the first system, and understanding that the future is uncertain are at the heart of the reasons for diversification. Diversification can be applied by trading a different asset class (for example, a stock v. a future), a different market (Crude Oil v. Gold or Soybeans), or trading the same market with a different trading system.

You now should have an idea of some of the underlying reasoning behind position sizing and diversification along with an understanding of what is realistically possible with a trading system.

Proper application of position sizing and diversification are key trading success factors. Before addressing more of the success factors relating to trading, the next few chapters will look at some of the factors that contribute to failure. I believe that by making you aware of them, you will have a deeper understanding of what it takes to be successful.

Resource: If you would like more information on trading systems similar to the system shown here visit www.automatedonlinetrading.com and check out the latest system updates.

Things to Remember

- Align your expectations of the years that it takes to learn how to trade well ... and how much money can be made with reality.

- Be wary of advertisements that make unrealistic claims and always require proof prior to purchase.

- Be aware of the positive impacts of position sizing on a system's performance but do not ignore the increased drawdown that will come with increased profit potential.

- Diversification is insurance against an uncertain world. Never put your eggs in one basket.

Chapter 3

Understanding an Unnatural World

This chapter is somewhat theoretical, but it will help you to understand the foundational concepts that underlie markets and trading. After all, how can you possibly beat the markets if you don't understand some underlying theories and concepts of the markets and the human factors that work against your success in markets?

The concept of 'randomness' of markets is not covered in many trading books – even the most popular ones – or in the courses that I attended early in my trading. I was studying trading for some time before becoming more aware of these concepts and understanding how they related to my initial trading results.

I firmly believe that:

The markets are overwhelmingly made up of random 'noise' **most** *of the time.*

I am not alone in this realization. This belief is based on two theories originated from extensive research by academics:

- Efficient Market Hypothesis (EMH) and
- Random Walk Hypothesis.

Now, if these two theories were 100% correct, you would (theoretically at least), not be able to make money trading the markets. Now, please stay with me on this.

Efficient Market Hypothesis

The Efficient Market Hypothesis (EMH) states that:

"A capital market is said to be efficient if it fully and correctly reflects all relevant information in determining security prices. Formally, the market is said to be efficient with respect to some information set if security prices would be unaffected by revealing that information to all participants. Moreover, efficiency with respect to an information set implies that it is impossible to make economic profits by trading on the basis of [that information set]." (Malkiel, 2007)

In brief, it says that markets take all available information both efficiently and correctly and that this information is immediately reflected in the price. Therefore, by strict interpretation, it would not be possible to make money based on that information, as in historical chart data, because it is already incorporated in prices.

So, the EMH concludes that it is virtually impossible to make money in markets based on analysis of historical data. This goes *totally* against the core of technical analysis, which is based on analysis of historical data.

There are three forms of the EMH:
- the weak form addresses only past prices,
- the semi-strong form includes all publicly-available information, and
- the strong form includes all information, even secret and insider information.

Most researchers determine that the strong form is somewhat contradicted by empirical evidence. However, the weak form is strongly supported.

Fortunately, the EMH is a model and, being a model, it represents a simplified representation of the real investing world, which is very complex. In order to simplify the model to represent a complex real world, certain assumptions have been made, which happen to be flawed.

Flawed assumptions made by the EMH include:

- All participants receive market information at the same time
- No frictions such as slippage and commissions, or finance costs apply. (If you have ever traded, you know that this is not true.)
- Everyone always acts rationally (This is obviously untrue. Even professionals do not always work without emotions when making trading decisions.)
- People never make mistakes. (Traders make mistakes. I can attest to that personally.)

However:

- Under-reactions and overreactions to news often occur (which contradicts the EMH's assertion that there is an immediate reflection of information)
- Information costs money – research costs, data access costs, etc.
- Inside information is not a factor (Ha! We know that insider trading does exist. This is confirmed by the news and by the SEC's efforts to combat it in the finance industry.)
- Long term mispricing - bubbles and busts - should not occur if the EMH were 100% correct.

Academic opinions may vary, but many researchers do believe that markets are indeed highly efficient and that this efficiency leads to the randomness of markets.

The books and courses I took did mention EMH at least briefly and it was typically dismissed outright. It is not necessary or appropriate for me as a trader to prove or disprove the EMH. Academia has dedicated the minds of people much smarter than

I to the development of the theory, and because of that, I don't believe it can be dismissed - at least, not fully.

However, I can look at the core assumptions of the EMH, combine them with my experience (and other traders' experiences) developing and trading systems and conclude, as others have,

- that the markets are in fact efficient *most of the time, but not all the time*
- therefore, there are opportunities to make money in markets at those times when a market is not efficient

Further: According to Dr. Andrew W. Lo, a Professor of Finance at the MIT Sloan School of Management, market efficiency is an evolving phenomenon. He has developed the Adaptive Market Hypothesis (AMH), which states that the efficiency of a market increases over time.

The implication being that newer markets will reach a level of efficiency over time, but initially there may be more opportunities in less traded and younger markets. Meaning that the S&P 500 Index may be an efficient market more often than the Hushen 300 Index (China), being a less traded, less mature market. AMH supports the concept that markets are not efficient all of the time.

Random Walk Hypothesis

Random Walk Hypothesis (RWH) states that market price changes are random and cannot be predicted.

It is a separate theory from EMH, and the EMH does not require or depend on the random walk hypothesis. But market randomness is consistent with the efficient market hypothesis.

RWH concludes that randomly evolving prices are the necessary consequence of intelligent investors competing to discover relevant information before the rest of the market becomes aware of it.

Again, we have a theory from academia that cannot be dismissed, at least not fully.

A trader needs to be aware and accept that most of the data on a chart is random, just as it must be accepted that, most of the time markets are efficient.

Importantly, those times when a market is inefficient and is not random represent an opportunity to make money.

That is why an edge is a critical success factor in trading. You need a proven edge to identify when the market is not efficient, and the data you are analysing is not just random market noise. (The job of the trading systems developer is to find times in the market when the data is not random and when money can be made.)

But, let's look at randomness a little closer. Randomness is one of the keys to understanding why there are so many failed traders. It is not the only critical factor, but it is important to be aware of it because it accounts for many incorrect analysis concepts and conclusions - not only in the trading world but also in daily life.

People have an inadequate intuition and perception of randomness. This inadequacy is a fundamental element of human perception. People can typically determine that something "can't be random" when it fact it is.

People do not perceive that random data can trend, and contain repeated patterns, but both price trends and repeatable price patterns occur in random data more than people think. Let's look at to two related cognitive biases that are rooted in our inherent inability to perceive random data.

The Hot Hand fallacy is the tendency to believe that, based on series or string of random events with the same successful outcome, the next random event has a higher chance of the *same* successful outcome. As it applies to trading, it is the belief that the next trade in a string of winning trades will have a higher chance of being a winning trade. This may sound like a relatively benign bias but, if you are a beginner discretionary trader who has not built a strong trading discipline through experience, you may be overconfident going into the next trade, causing you to make mistakes.

The Gamblers Fallacy is potentially much more destructive. This is the tendency to believe that, based on a series or string of events, the next event to occur has a higher chance of the *opposite* result. If, for example, you're in Las Vegas playing roulette and the wheel has hit on black the last five times, you bet on red because you feel it is due to land on red next - but that is not actually the case.

This fallacy is rooted in a misinterpretation of the mathematical concept of 'regression to the mean' that dictates that over a large number of coin flips, you will have an equal number of heads and tails. People typically feel that after a long series of coin flips that result in heads, that a series of tails is due. It may not be true and is flawed reasoning.

If a coin is flipped and it results in heads for five flips out of ten, the next flip has a 50/50 chance of being heads. If a coin is flipped 100 times and 75 of the flips are heads, perhaps you do not have a fair coin (a coin that results in a 50/50 distribution of wins to losses). Like Las Vegas, trading is a numbers game.

In trading systems, you do not want to trade a 'fair coin'; you need to have a statistical edge. Casinos in Las Vegas make money because they have an edge. For any game, they know that, over a series of bets, the result will be positive for the casino. Trading also requires identifying such edges that, over a series of trades, demonstrate that the outcome will be positive for the trader.

In trading, this fallacy is the very common. Many hold the account-depleting belief that each time you experience a losing trade, the chances that the next trade will be a winner are better. In fact, if you are trading a system that does not have a known edge, your chances will be 50/50. As in a coin flip, the odds will not increase in your favour with each losing trade.

Think about how just these biases can affect a trader's interpretation of their trading results and their decisions. Like me, you may have experienced these biases yourself. However, there are more, and they are discussed later in chapter 5.

A favourite work of mine, which is included in my recommended reading list, is *Fooled by Randomness*, by Nicholas Taub. In this book, he demonstrates that even logical, educated people fail to understand randomness. Being logical and well educated may make matters worse in regards to your perception of randomness.

If you have taken trading courses, you will have seen the disclaimers required by government regulatory agencies (See examples in Appendix I – The Usual Disclaimers).

You should now understand the reason for this common disclaimer excerpt:

"The past performance of any trading system or methodology is not necessarily indicative of future results."

In a world of randomness and uncertainty this fully applies. With that in mind, when you are in a world of markets that are mostly random, statistical and probability analysis is your best ally. It is the 'friend' that enables you to analyse mostly random markets and evaluate system performance and trading results.

Things to Remember

- Markets are efficient most of the time and markets price changes are random most of the time.

- When a market is efficient or random, you will not be able to make money.

- Statistical analysis of data is required to identify those times when a market is not random.

- Identification of an edge is necessary to take advantage of those non-random price movements in a market.

- Never forget that the markets are mostly random and, therefore, uncertain. Success is based on maximizing probabilities. Realizing that makes living with trading much easier.

Chapter 4

Technical Analysis ... or Reading Tea Leaves?

Technical analysis is a method of analysing a chart of a stock, futures or forex prices and volume, and applying a set of tools to identify patterns that reveal a probability of the future action of price.

There are two major issues with technical analysis.

a) many of the tools are subjective,
b) some tools are not statistically significant

If you read books on trading or wandered the internet to learn more about trading, you may be surprised by what I will cover in this section.

Much of the tools of technical analysis are based on trading lore and not scientific study to determine whether they are statistically significant and contribute to you having an edge in the market.

Subjectivity

Popular technical analysis includes tools such as hand-drawn trendlines, support and resistance levels, Elliot Wave Principle, Gann Patterns. If you have looked into trading at all, you are probably aware of some of these tools.

The issue with many of these tools is that they are subjective. If you gave the same chart to five different chart analysts, each would analyse the chart data and could reach different conclusions.

Since they are subjective and do not define an exact method of application, these methods cannot be rigorously tested to prove that they reliably provide a significant edge. Their probabilities cannot be tested. Yet, these methods are taught as though they were a religion. You are meant to simply have faith that they work.

Well, I need more than faith to put my money on the line, and so should you.

Lack of statistical significance

Other technical analysis tools, such as 'moving averages' and Fibonacci retracements, may not be subjective in their application, but it must be proven that they provide a significant edge. In the case of, for example, Fibonacci levels, I have yet to see a study showing that they provide any significant edge.

When I first started trading, I was taught about Fibonacci Ratios. I was quite enamoured with them and that fact they were found in nature, architecture and all the usual claims. I was taught to look for retracements in pullbacks to Fibonacci levels such as 61.8%, 38.2%, 23.2%. (Oddly enough, they also reference 50% as a retracement level, which is not a Fibonacci level.)

This was part of my Elliot Wave training as provided by the options TEP and other training providers, and books that I read. I would also use 'fib' ratios as inputs to my indicators, as recommended by my instructors.

Fibonacci Retracements

I mentioned that I had yet to see a study proving that Fibonacci levels are indeed relevant in trading, which is true. On the other hand, Adam H. Grimes, in his study of statistical significance of popular technical tools (moving averages, Fib ratios, etc.), determined that Fibonacci ratios do NOT accurately reflect the retracements in markets. The study concluded that there was no evidence of that typical Fibonacci levels provided any edge.

The case goes back to the randomness of markets. You may have had a run of wins based on entries at Fibonacci retracement levels, but that was due to the randomness of markets, not because the Fibonacci numbers are actually significant.

Several other studies address the usefulness of Fibonacci levels. Conclusions of two of them are presented below.

a) *"While there was limited evidence that Fibonacci retracements exerted predictive power over exchange rates, the magnitude of this power was minimal (at most 4%). Noting that statistical significance does not confer economic relevance, the author of this paper is extremely sceptical that Fibonacci ratios can be used to generate significant risk-adjusted returns in currency markets"* (Gupta, 2011)

b) *"The empirical result we obtained does appear to corroborate the claim of technical analysts that there is some predictive utility associated with Fibonacci sequences used as filters in automated trading systems. However, we must add that this is merely indicative and by no means conclusive empirical evidence and more exhaustive studies are required before any definite conclusion can be drawn."* (Bhattacharya & Kumar, 2006)

Another teaching in technical analysis is that the shallower a retracement, the stronger the extension or continuation leg of the trend. It was also contradicted by a study that concluded that shallower retracements leading to stronger extensions is not supported by statistical analysis of market data across three asset classes - Equities, Futures and Forex.

Moving Averages

Other common technical analysis concepts that are unsupported by statistical analysis of the data include the relevance of 'special' moving averages used as support and resistance and the use of moving averages to determine trend direction.

Some conclusions based on analysis of moving averages for statistical significance were:

- There are no special moving averages (length)
- Moving averages do not provide for reliable support
- The slope of a moving average is not a reliable indicator of trend
- Trend indicators derived from the position of multiple moving averages are not reliable indicators of the trend.

Many technical analysis books also teach that the same technical analysis tools apply to any asset class. I have seen this to be untrue in my system's development and analysis.

Just because one technical analysis tool or indicator works in the equity or stock market, it does not mean it will work in the same way and with similar results in futures or forex markets.

Be wary of unsubstantiated claims of any trading indicator, methodology or system offering that promises successful trading without the proof of its historical performance, addressed further in upcoming chapters.

Things to Remember

- Subjective technical analysis tools cannot be adequately tested and should not be used by traders.

- Many technical analysis tools may seem to result in successful trading for a time, but that may be due simply due to random market data and will not perform over the long term.

- Do your research. There are books and courses that analyse different technical analysis tools to determine their statistical edge if any. Find out what works.

- Be wary of unproven trading tools (books, indicators, systems). Proof of performance is not demonstrated by a few successful trade examples.

Chapter 5

Where Anyone Can Go Wrong

Many traders have met with the challenges addressed here, as have I. Be optimistic! You need to be aware of them so that you can be ready for success.

Under-capitalization

When I first started in trading automated systems, I traded futures systems I had purchased from a system vendor.

Like many other system vendors, this one focused on the margin requirements as the basis for the account size needed to trade his systems. Think of margin as a good-faith deposit set by the exchange and the broker as being the amount of capital you required to trade the system. However, the amount of money you'll need in your account to *safely* trade any system *must* be based on a statistical analysis (see chapter 11 Monte Carlo Analysis) of the historical performance of that system over time. The vendor did not provide this and, at the time; I was not aware enough to ask.

As a result, my account was underfunded. I did not have enough in the account to protect me from the inevitable drawdown.

For example, to trade one contract of the E-mini S&P 500 futures at Interactive Brokers, (as of June 2015) you must have a minimum of $2875 in your account to initiate an intraday trade, $5750 to enter a trade in the overnight market session. Margin increases when you hold overnight due to the higher risk.

Many discount brokers promote their low margin rates to attract traders. Here are a couple of examples:

- A "Discount Emini Broker" with $400 Margins and a free trading platform
- Others offer $300 day-trading margins for the E-mini S&P, E-mini NASDAQ and the E-mini Dow Jones futures per contract

Wow! What a great deal! I can start trading right away!

They offer these rates to attract a steady wave of new day-traders who have got their hands on a trading approach or system and are not aware of and/or do not have the money to adequately fund their account for the system they are trading.

Brokers do this because, no matter what, they will get their money. The commissions will keep rolling in per trade. When they let you trade the E-mini S&P with only $400 per contract in your account, and you are suddenly down $800 that day (a typical daily move being $750 to $1000 per contract),

- your account is frozen from any trading and
- you receive a very abrupt phone call demanding the difference.

But three or four hundred dollars per contract is far from the actual minimum capital required if you want to survive trading ANY futures trading system.

Even Interactive Brokers rates may not be sufficient to sustain your trading system. It all depends on the system's maximum drawdown and the analysis of it.

Lack of knowledge

It may seem obvious, but too many traders jump into the business without the prerequisite knowledge to survive and be successful. Trading requires awareness, knowledge, application and balancing of many subject areas, as well as discipline and commitment. Entry into the field should not be taken lightly or by the unprepared.

People are sometimes seduced by the fact that it's so exciting and easy to start. After all, what other business has such a low cost of entry? Not many, but not many have such a high rate of failure.

In my experience, the problem with trading is that you don't know what you don't know. As former United States Secretary of Defense Donald Rumsfeld once told journalists:

> *There are known knowns. These are things we know that we know.*
> *There are known unknowns. That is to say, there are things that we know we don't know. But there are also unknown unknowns. There are things we don't know we don't know.*

What seems at first a nonsensical statement (especially from the Secretary of Defense) does have some merit in that what you are not aware of; you cannot prepare for. As mentioned previously, it is best to know so you can be ready.

As an example, you may be trading a system with a proven edge and performance history, but if you are not aware of the effect that cognitive biases can have on your live trading decisions and how to manage them, your results will not meet the expectations set by the system's history.

Over-expectations

Although discussed earlier, I just want to remind new traders to be wary of advertisements (you'll see an actual example in a later chapter):

- focusing on winning trades,

- showing high percentage win-rates,
- indicating large amounts of money can be made in a short time
- featuring all other headlines that vendors use as magnets to excite potential customers looking to make a killing in the markets.

If you are serious about learning about and being successful in trading, don't curb your enthusiasm. Keep your expectations based in reality, which is one of the things I hope this book helps you to do.

Underestimated Learning Curve

You cannot look at your success in your career or your level of education to forecast how successful you will be in learning about, or undertaking, trading.

Many highly educated and skilled professionals, such as doctors, lawyers, engineers, enter the world of trading and fall flat on their face. They often enter the trading arena with the idea that they can emulate their great success in the past and be able to apply themselves to trading and achieve the same level of success. As I was once told: "Really, it can't be harder than learning to be a doctor, can it?"

Well, 'yes' and 'no' because some the skills you need to become a successful trader are very different from the skills necessary to become a successful doctor, lawyer, engineer, etc.

Cognitive biases

Cognitive biases influence how we think. They can lead to errors in decisions and judgments.

Trading requires very different thinking – thinking in ways that are new to many people and are not in sync with the standard ways that humans think of and experience the day-to-day world.

Many cognitive biases exist in human nature, and they will certainly work against you in the world of trading. To be a successful trader, you must learn to counteract these natural tendencies, along with learning the new skills required for success.

You have already been introduced to two of the many cognitive biases that can work against you – the Hot Hand and Gamblers Fallacies. Let's now look at other common biases that can negatively affect your trading; as they did mine when I was starting out.

Overconfidence bias is common belief that we are better than average in just about anything. A vast majority of people feel they are better than the average person when it comes to driving, or cooking, or whatever the case. However, this cannot be true for everyone because the average is well, average.

In general, people think they are better traders than they indeed are … and are better traders than the average trader. Some of us may believe that have an exceptional intelligence, an unusual skill or perhaps intuition when it comes to trading. They may also be over-confident in their trading system or the extent that they believe markets are predictable.

Overconfidence is the enemy of successful trading.

Imagine that you are a discretionary trader following an Elliot Wave-based approach (NOT recommended), and you've just had a string of wins. Now, you are feeling very confident – so confident, for the next trade, you decide that you will buy 1000 shares instead of your usual 500 shares, expecting to make double the profit. After all, you have this Elliot Wave thing down. What could go wrong?

Except that it does go wrong, and you lose twice as much money on this trade … and that is if you were experienced enough to get out at a predetermined stop loss. (More on stop-losses later). If not, you may have just wiped out your earlier profits. Note how this situation also relates to the Hot Hand bias in the randomness section.

Learn to be humble when it comes to trading. Realize that trading is a world of uncertainty and you don't know where the market will go. You can only maximize the probabilities by having a rigorously tested trading system with a statistical edge - something many traders don't have.

Loss aversion or risk bias is the tendency for people
- to prefer to take a guaranteed profit, or
- to hold onto a loss in the hope that it will result in a gain eventually.

People hate to lose in any situation, not just in trading. This innate flaw is rooted in our emotion brain. The pain of any loss will register much more powerfully than the pleasure associated with a gain. In fact, some psychologists have reported that a loss levies an emotional impact 2.5 times greater than the pleasure of a gain.

This explains why a beginning trader will enter a trade, such as a trend trade, and instead of sticking with the trading plan and staying in the trade in order to maximize profits, the trader will exit as soon as the trade's profits start to decrease. Alternatively, they may exit as soon as there is some small profit in the trade, which is fatal in trend trading where losing trades far outnumber winners … and the fewer winning trades must make enough money to compensate for the larger number of losing trades. (This the basis of the overused trading axiom "let your profits run", applying to trend-following trades.)

The other manifestation of this bias is holding on to a losing trade and hoping, hoping, hoping that it turns around and becomes a winner - even as the loss continues to get worse and worse.

It has happened to me and many other traders and probably has happened to you if you've traded in the past.

Although it is simple to counter this particular bias, the effects of other biases often affect your trading judgement. So, you will need to have a good plan and stick to it.

That plan is your trading system (and the discipline to stick to it). It is unconditionally a crucial key to success.

Confirmation bias is our tendency to give more weight to data and information that support or confirm our existing beliefs while consciously or unconsciously ignoring contradicting data.

We also tend to surround ourselves with others who share similar beliefs. This is reflected in social media, workplaces, professional and academic societies, and political and religious groups. There is nothing inherently wrong with that, except when it comes to decision making.

Look at this scenario. You are a trader in a losing long position, you check your indicators, you scour the news looking for information to support your position, to prove you are right ... but the market is going the 'wrong way'. Suffering from confirmation bias, most of the time you will end up experiencing more and more losses as the reality of the situation overcomes your cognitive bias.

Initially, I was not immune to this. Earlier in my trading history, as I mentioned, I suffered from indicator fascination when analysing stocks. I would even add indicators to give me more 'insight' when all they did was produce more ambiguity.

Today, I am somewhat anti-indicator, and only use those few

that I have proven to have an edge in my trading systems. Confirmation bias can be avoided by being aware of it and being open to inputs that contradict your point of view. As it applies to trading, you can fight it by:

- Knowing your risk before you enter a trade and setting a point where you accept that the market is going against your trade and take a manageable and acceptable loss, remembering losing trades are a cost of doing business.

- We like to win and are taught from childhood to feel our best when we are right, but in trading you need to fight the need to be right all the time. Understand that a trading system with a 30% win rate can make a lot of money.

- Remember that trading is a world of uncertainty. No method of trading is infallible, nor is it absolute.

- Don't focus on why a trade has gone wrong (lost money). Be satisfied that you executed the trade as per your plan and got out at your stop loss.

Hindsight Bias is dubbed the "I knew it all along" bias by psychologists. An event, such as a losing trade entry, can look much clearer in hindsight, and you may over-simplify the reasons why you took the trade and why it resulted in a loss.

It's the "would've, should've, could've" syndrome, which we have all experienced.

This especially is an issue if you are using subjective criteria to enter a trade; and more so if you are using multiple criteria such as indicators or chart drawings or indeed any criteria that does not have an 'edge'.

This bias leads to dangerous overconfidence, which can lead the trader to believe they can predict the future of the market with some level of control over the market. Both notions are far from the truth.

Once again, we return to the effects of market randomness, as previous trades based on random market data will always look less random than they were.

Overcoming this is as previously discussed. Be humble. Have a proven edge in the market you are trading that performs better than the performance of the same edge on random data.

Anchoring Bias is our tendency to put too much weight on data based on some initial event and to base our future decisions too heavily on that data. First impressions tend to have a greater impact on us, and act as an anchor with which we retain our future decisions. This anchored data may be only loosely related to a current decision, and may even be irrelevant to it, but we may make a decision based on it regardless.

Here is a scenario. You are a discretionary day trader trading the SPI futures, and the session starts out with a strong bullish move. You feel excited about the now-expected upward trending day ahead and are convinced of its inevitability.

However, despite failed entry after failed entry, you do not realise that the initial bullish move was in reality a sign of the exhaustion of a trend, not the start of a new one. By the end of the day, after a string of losing trades, you finally do recognise that you incorrectly misinterpreted the market. You did so because you were anchored by that initial bullish move and made all of your subsequent trading decisions based on that move.

A discretionary trader would advise that you must constantly and consistently follow the flow of the market and make trading decisions based on what the market is telling you currently. However, while technical analysis relies on the analysis of historical data, you must avoid holding on to past conclusions.

Anchoring bias is also used against you in marketing. You may have seen advertisements from training providers and system vendors that have visuals of charts with fantastic winning trades, to which you will naturally anchor. Marketers know this and the extent to which it will influence your buying decision in their favour. Having a mechanical plan, i.e. a mechanical trading system helps to manage this bias, as well as others.

Recency Bias is our tendency to rely on our recent experiences as a reference for what may occur in the future … as opposed to relying on experiences further back into the past. Although this bias is not a problem most of the time, it can certainly become a problem in trading or investment.

Suppose you are trading a trend trading system, which has a 50% win rate. In such a system, there is the probability of experiencing losing streaks of between 5 to 18 trades in a row.

During one of these losing streaks, you may start to feel that the system will never provide another win. So you turn it off and stop trading it. The next time it trades it produces a huge win, but you missed it.

You should know the characteristics of your trading system including the potential numbers of losses in a row, and being able to recognise a statistically-based point that tells you whether the system is performing within its normal operating parameters.

If it is not, have a predefined set of criteria that assist you when making the decision to stop trading it.

Another example – one that I suffered – was back in 2008-2009 when my superannuation account was tied to the US S&P 500.

Because of the market's volatility, I changed to basic interest bearing and, luckily, did not have any catastrophic losses in the crash.

BUT, because the market was going south for so long (and because of my recency bias), I was convinced it would never recover. So, I missed out on a lot of potential profits because, even when it started to go up, I didn't believe it would continue.

I did not change it back to the S&P 500 until well into the recovery and the market uptrend that is still under way at the time of writing.

It is very easy to forget the market's cycles and even the characteristics of a system we are actively trading. Markets that go down will go back up. I should have been more aware and have had a plan in place to deal with a confirmed uptrend that was going to happen, sooner or later.

In my early trading experience, this bias resulted in me jumping from one trading technique to another. Because of recent experiences of losing trades using a pullback entry method, I jumped to a breakout entry technique - even though I had experience of winning trades from the pullback technique. This happened to me and happens to many other beginner traders as they jump from technique to technique. You can see how the Loss Aversion and Recency biases work hand in hand in this case.

Being aware of the bias itself and being open to, and planning for potential outcomes is how you can minimize the effects of this, and any cognitive bias.

Illusion of control is a bias that causes you to believe that you have a level of influence over an event or outcome when, in reality, you have no control or influence whatsoever. Gambling games, like slot machines, provide good examples.

Your trading system may give you the illusion of control. Your charting system or trading platform may contribute to the feeling of control of the market.

As you have read previously, early on I bought a charting program with all the usual indicators, including Elliot Wave analysis, Fibonacci levels and the like. I felt as if I were able to control the market. However, the reality of my results showed that I was wrong.

This may sound like heresy but you cannot control (or predict) the market.

And, it's not just you. No one, no matter what they may say, can predict the markets. In trading, you enter the 'domain of the uncertain'. It is beyond your control. Learn to be comfortable with its uncertainty and concentrate on those aspects of trading that you can control - such as your emotions, your actions and your mind. Although not easy, it is more achievable than trying to control the markets.

You have probably noted how two or more of these biases can join forces to work against you ... and there are more biases out there. I've chosen the above set because I have experienced dealing with them personally and so can relate to each of them.

Most of these biases cannot be overcome, as they are innate, fundamental elements of each of us. As in the past, they are useful in our everyday life situations and typically are not a problem. In regards to trading, the best we can do is manage them.

To manage them, you must be aware of them and understand that they exist. You have already taken the first step by reading this chapter. I encourage you to research them, to think about them, and expand your knowledge of them.

You will need to apply your knowledge of the biases when you make any important decision, especially ones that are made under pressure, or involve high risk, or involve a lot of emotions for you. This really has applied to every investment decision that I have made in recent years.

As my pursuit of trading knowledge continued, I became increasingly aware of the presence of biases. Initially, I was unable to instantly counteract their effects on my trading, but over time I have learned how to deal with them.

When you are under the pressure of making trading decisions, all the biases raise their ugly heads, and that is when mistakes are made, and money is lost. You have to fight these biases throughout your trading career, but it does get easier with experience.

This is one of the reasons I pursued system trading, then automated system trading, because it eliminates the execution errors attributed to the biases. However, automation does not avoid the effects of all of them.

As mentioned previously, you need to have the discipline to follow the system 100%, although there will be times when the biases will taunt you not to do so.

Ask yourself regularly, "Am I being influenced by any bias?" Are your thoughts or perceptions being overly swayed by one of these cognitive biases?

In trading, these biases are mitigated to a certain degree, by having a well-designed mechanical trading system and plan that includes statistical analysis of your trading results. And, of course, don't forget the required discipline to follow it.

Managing these biases does take some serious time and effort. Let's face it, being a human is a tough gig sometimes ... and trading can make it tougher when proceeding unprepared.

Things to Remember

- Accept that successful trading requires a learning curve, typically longer than you want it to be as there are many aspects of trading that must be learned to be proficient.

- Trading is not just about learning the skills to know when to place entry and exit orders. It's about knowing, and having confidence in, every aspect of the method based on its performance history, and forming a plan so that you can properly manage your trading and the emotions and cognitive biases that work against you.

- Cognitive biases are a part of being human and affect everyone to a certain degree.

- If you have experience trading, think about how each bias may have affected your performance.

- System trading can mitigate many of the biases to a certain degree.

- Continue learning about cognitive biases through your further research.

Chapter 6

Success Factors

After addressing a range of trading failure factors for some time, you will probably be relieved that we are now turning to trading success. After all, that is what you want to achieve.

Trade categories

Let's look first at trade categories. They can help to simplify how you look at trading and the types of trades and trading systems available to you, and hopefully will help you to understand some of the confusing terms in the trading world.

Directional trading systems execute trades in one of the two following trade categories:

Mean Reversion trade category attempts to take advantage of a market where significant price moves are reversed. The trade is entered in opposition to the trend on that particular timeframe. Typically after a large move with the trend, a market will revert to the mean or reverse from that recent high.

With-trend trade category attempts to take advantage of a market where large price movements create momentum that leads to more movement in the same direction. The trade is entered in the same direction as the trend and momentum in that particular timeframe.

A with-trend trade may seek to stay in a trend lasting several weeks for multiple trend legs until it reverses ... or it may be active only for a single swing of a trend, downward or upward, lasting only a few days, hours or even minutes.

No matter what the trade, it will fall into one of these two types. They are important because while these market forces occur in all asset classes, one may occur more often in one than the other.

In general, data analysis shows that equities tend to have a stronger tendency towards mean reversion mode when compared with futures and forex asset classes. It doesn't mean that equities, don't trend. They do. It means that mean reversion happens more in that asset class than others.

Alternately, the futures and forex asset classes have a strong tendency towards with-trend or trend-following than equities. It is one reason trading methods that work on one asset class may not work on another. I would not recommend trading a mean-reversion trading system that works well in equities in forex, for example.

Note that the strength of these overall tendencies can vary with the specific market within an asset class and the timeframe being traded.

It is the goal of any trading system to identify which of these forces are dominant, to define the edge and to take advantage of that dominant force with the appropriate trade.

Having a proven edge

The number one success factor is that you have an established edge and the primary factor behind any trading decision should always be based on your edge in a given market.

The proof of such an edge is sufficient trade history on which you can create performance parameters and statistics for evaluation of the trading strategy. The criteria are covered later in the 'Assessing a system' chapters.

System trading

System trading is the application of a mechanical set of trading rules. It may also be referred to as systematic trading, algorithmic trading or strategy trading.

It defines the exact prerequisites and criteria for entering each trade ... and for exiting each trade as well. There is no variation from the rule set. Every trade is entered and exited on the same rules.

For reference, mechanical is defined as (an action) done without thought or spontaneity; being automatic, machinelike, unthinking, unemotional, unconscious, involuntary, instinctive, routine, matter-of-fact, habitual, inattentive.

Whether the trading system is being executed by a computer or a human, the definition of mechanical applies.

When I use the term *system trading*, I am referring to a mechanical trading system. There is no discretion involved.

- You do not stop trading the system because a financial report is scheduled for release on a particular day (unless it is an integral part of your system), or if you have some 'intuitive' feeling not to take the trade.

- You do not modify the exit criteria because you 'feel' that it would be beneficial to do so. Your feelings do not apply.

- If you are watching the market of the specific trade and some aspect of it causes you to feel anxiety, fear, or greed, you stay the course.

- The system is applied 100% of the time, and there is no variation from it.

As long as the system is performing within its expected performance profile, which is reflected in its equity curve and performance parameters, it's on and ready to go without deviation from the rules set. It is an important aspect of system trading that many traders do not adhere to because it's not easy to do so.

Believe me, I've done it and learned the lesson. There is nothing worse than looking at winning trades that you have missed ... profits you could have booked, but you missed because you stopped following the system for some reason.

For me, this is extremely aggravating ... and I am happy to have moved beyond the temptation.

Why is this so important? It is vital because, for a reliable, robustly-developed system, you must have all of the contingencies covered.

- Your system, if properly developed, is based on years of data and a proven statistical edge in the market you are trading. The analysis has been done, and the results quantified.

- You have a plan, based on the analysis of all the system performance parameters. You know what results to expect. You know how your system is performing and if it is healthy.

- Variations from your system will distort the results of your system, and the more you deviate from the system, the more it will be distorted and 'out of sync' with your tested system.

- You will no longer be able to assess the current performance of your system and know that it is performing as expected, based on all of the previous analysis.

So, to ensure your success as a system trader, you must commit to this 100%.

System trading v. discretionary

Discretionary trading is an alternative approach to the systems trading method. With it, the discretionary trader decides which trades to take on an individual basis, based on the most current information available.

While discretionary traders may follow a trading system with a pre-defined clear set of rules, they may use their own discretion to vary the rules - based on their interpretation of chart data or due so some other reason, which may be subjective, like intuition. In fact, their trading approach may be wholly based on subjective interpretations of data.

While many system traders consider discretionary trading to be a 'dead end', there are several outstanding successful discretionary traders including Paul Tudor Jones and Louis Bacon.

To be 100% discretionary in your trading does not make sense to me, and you should never base your trades solely on intuition or any subjective method that can be influenced by emotions.

Some traders believe that a hybrid of the two disciplines does make sense, although I am not convinced as yet. But I do believe there may be an artful side to trading.

Over years of chart analysis and experience trading markets, one could build up an intuition. Combining that intuition with rules that are based on a proven edge - as applied exclusively by a systems trader – could be very successful in trading. The problem is the time that it takes build such intuition and experience and whether the hybrid method will work for you in the long run. Many system traders cringe at the thought of combining the two methods.

In professional circles, the number of system traders far exceeds the number of discretionary traders. Professional system traders also control a larger number of assets than discretionary traders, and the longevity of systems traders tends to be greater than that of discretionary traders.

Systems traders concentrate on identifying the periods when market price data is not random and the market moves enough to make it worthwhile to attempt to make money during a non-random data period, as demonstrated by historical data analysis.

The bottom line here is that, if you want the highest probability of success in trading, you need an objective, logical, mechanical approach.

You need to be a systems trader, and you need criteria to judge the merits of any system you are considering to trade. (See chapters 8 – 11)

Risk management

Risk management is implemented through the consistent application of stop losses in any system you trade. Managing drawdown by applying Monte Carlo analysis to determine minimum starting account size (proper capitalization), cease-trading account levels, risk of ruin and mean drawdown analysis is, in my view, the key to successful trading. It helps to lower the degree of uncertainty when trading a system evaluated using Monte Carlo simulation (see chapter 11).

Position sizing

Sometimes called 'money management', position sizing defines, in the case of futures, how many contracts will be traded for any given trade. Many position sizing models are available. As you would have read earlier, it would be a 'crime' to trade a rigorously tested, proven system with only a single contract. To do so would leave profit on the table and out of your reach.

The key is to use the lowest risk approach, typically based on using profits. Any position-sizing strategy should be pre-analysed and qualified by Monte Carlo simulation prior to your implementation of it. It should start small with 1-2 contracts in the case of a futures system, minimizing risk, adding contracts using profits and reducing contracts when the system is in a drawdown period. Like any component of a trading system, it is vital to stick to it and not to vary from the rules.

Psychology

There seems to be a great emphasis (perhaps over-emphasis?) on the psychology of trading. There is no doubt that mental attitude is a major factor in success. However, no amount of mental preparation will help you if you don't first employ a trading system with a tested and proven edge; a system that has been developed and evaluated properly.

From my perspective, risk acceptance is the biggest mental hurdle for a new trader. It is vitally as important to acknowledge and be aware of the drawdown of a system as the potential profits of any trading approach.

Risk and reward go hand in hand. So, smile and embrace drawdown. All trading systems have drawdown. The key is to be aware of the drawdown of your particular system ... and know that you can mentally manage it.

Vision, planning and record keeping

Also key to success in trading is to have a clear vision and a plan with specific goals for how to achieve the vision. Most people start out with a very unrealistic vision and plan for easy big money in a short time, as I did. However, I did commit to not giving up from the very start.

My vision eventually evolved to successfully and confidently trading multiple instruments and robust, reliable, consistently profitable systems automatically. My plan mapped out the steps I needed to take to get there. It took years, and the plan evolved, but I did achieve my vision.

Record keeping is also vital. I keep a daily diary notating details of each trade, and my trading emotions at the time. To be successful in anything (and trading is no different), you need a history of

- what has worked,
- what you have done right,
- what you have done wrong
- ... and how to fix it

It also helps to monitor your trading emotions. I like to track the market conditions versus my level of belief and confident in a system I'm trading. Such records to manage those cognitive biases you read about earlier. Drawdown periods can be tough.

So, always keep a diary of your trading-related activities *and* emotions.

Commitment and discipline

Any type of trading requires a significant commitment and investment of your time, effort and focus as trading is not a trivial affair - as much of the general public believes. While trading in its essence may be simple, it is a challenging endeavour and requires discipline to maintain your commitment to achieving the competence you desire.

It takes a clear vision, combined with your commitment, to maintain your strength, and establish the discipline to create and stick to your plan.

So, establish the discipline of keeping a daily diary, keep your vision in mind, keep learning, and make the commitment to stay the course even when things don't go your way, which will happen. Sometimes often.

Things to Remember

- Market movements and thus directional trades are either With-trend or Mean Reverting.

- System trading maximizes your probability of success in trading.

- BE A SYSTEMS TRADER.

- Evaluate your vision and commitment to trading and consistently build your discipline.

- Keep a daily log of your trading activities including your emotions at the time.

- Don't give up! Stay persistent in your trading efforts and you will find success.

Chapter 7

Asset Classes - A Quick Look

An asset class is a group of securities that have similar financial characteristics, behave similarly in the marketplace, and are subject to the same laws and regulations. As discussed previously, asset classes also have tendencies to favour a particular market force (Trending or Mean-Reverting).

Although much can be written about asset classes and definitions vary, from my perspective and experience, there are three primary asset classes for traders:

- equities,
- futures
- forex

Futures are my preferred trading vehicle, and what I now primarily trade.

Equities

Like many traders, I started my trading 'career' with equities. Equities are stocks. Often they are just called shares because that is what they are; a share in the ownership of a company, even if it is only a very minute fraction. Legally, you have an 'equity stake' in a corporation's assets.

Typically, stocks are purchased in a particular company like Microsoft or Cisco in the hope that, if the corporation is successful, other investors want to will pay an even higher price for them. If the owner of the shares then sells them at the higher price, they will produce a profit for them. Traders also look for returns in the shorter term by day trading or swing trading stocks, taking advantage of shorter directional moves.

Leverage lowers the initial costs of entry and provides increased potential for profit. Available in different forms, dependent on what is being traded, leverage involves

- the use of borrowed capital like 'margin' in the case of stocks, or
- certain types of financial instruments, such as derivatives - options or futures.

When managed accordingly, particularly avoiding over-leverage, it can be very desirable. Beware! Over-leverage is dangerous and can wipe you out in the event of a significant market downturn.

In a stock purchase, the margin is a loan that enables the investor to borrow up to 50% of the purchase price of shares. This is 2:1 leverage and is common in equities.

Let's say you are a day trader and XYZ stock is now trading at $50 per share.

Your goal is to make $5 (per share) on XYZ today, a five-point move.

- You purchase 100 shares at $50 for a total cost of $5,000, using the available balance in your broker account.
- The stock goes up, and you sell at $55.
- Your 100 shares are now worth $5,500.
- Ignoring broker commission and slippage for the moment, you have a gross profit of $500.

Using the same scenario, but if you now bought 200 shares for $10,000, using $5,000 from your account with the broker plus a 50% margin loan for the balance. You sell at $55, and now you have a gross profit of $1,000 – double the profit compared with not using margin.

However, let's say you don't have $5,000 available, and you don't have a margin loan available, how else could you take advantage of the 5-point move in XYZ?

Taking our hypothetical further, you could purchase a call option and control 200 XYZ shares for around $500 and make money off the same move in XYZ. Stock options are a leveraged product and like futures, are derivatives. The value of the stock option is derived from another asset, in this case, the stock.

Just by buying a single stock option, you can control 100 stock shares, for a fraction of the cost of buying the same stocks outright. Options are a complicated subject and beyond the scope of this book. I started trading stocks initially and was drawn to stock options because of their leverage and the low entry cost. Options are an excellent trading vehicle that I still use sometimes and have taught classes about trading with them.

However, once I discovered futures and linked them to automated trading, I decided to focus primarily on this asset class. I decided this because, in my opinion, futures have simplicity, provide leverage and are also easily traded via automated trading platforms.

What are futures?

Futures are contracts for a physical commodity or a financial instrument that obligate the buyer to buy, or the seller to sell, specific quantities at a specified price on a predetermined date. Futures contracts have set expiry dates - some monthly, some quarterly, and others at varying frequencies over the year. The specifications of each contract are available online on the website of the exchange where the contract is traded.

Futures are traded on central financial exchanges in most countries. The exchanges design each futures contract and its specifications and manage the marketplace for trading them.

All activity is regulated by the watchful eye of the government. For example, exchanges are governed in the USA by the Commodity Futures Trading Commission (CTFC), in Australia by the Australian Securities and Investment Commission (ASIC), in the U.K. by the Financial Services Authority (FSA), to name a few. These governing agencies have the authority to levy fines and other punishments on traders, individuals or companies who violate any of the rules.

Each futures contract specifies the quality and quantity of the underlying physical commodity or financial product. Physical commodity futures represent items you typically interact with on a daily basis. They are, for example, the wheat in food products, lumber used in building homes, gold in your jewellery, cotton in your clothing, gasoline and oil for your car. Financial products include currencies like the Euro, Swiss Franc, Australian dollar, US dollar or financial indexes like the S&P 500, Russell 2000, SPI 200 and many more.

A futures contract is settled at the contract expiry date on a cash basis or by physical delivery of the underlying asset. As such, a futures trader needs to be aware of the delivery type for the futures contract being traded, along with the expiry date. Otherwise, if you are still active in a futures contract with Settlement by physical delivery, you may find yourself with the annoying problem of having, say, 42,000 gallons of heating oil on its way to you with the accompanying balance due (See Table 1 below). Fortunately, in practice, brokers typically have policies in place to avoid such occurrences, and so you need to know what they are and manage your trading accordingly.

Futures contracts are highly leveraged. Meaning that you can buy a futures contract representing a much greater amount of the asset value than buying the straight share contract. It also means that a relatively slight movement of the futures contract price can result in a much greater dollar gain or loss for the trader.

Compared with equities with 2:1 leverage available through a margin loan, US futures contracts are commonly structured with much higher leverage. On average 5 to15:1 (or 5 to15% of a contract's value based on the size of the contract – See Table 1.)

For example, if you are a trader who wants to buy a single contract of gold (as you believe gold will go up in the next month or so), the gold futures contract is traded on the COMEX (Commodity Exchange, Inc). Each contract controls ten troy ounces of gold. So, with a margin requirement of $4,125, if you have that sum available in your account, you can purchase the contract.

If the price of gold is $1500.50 at the time you buy your one contract, you now control 100 troy ounces, $150,050 worth of gold with only a $4,125 margin requirement. With a minimum price fluctuation of $0.10 per troy ounce at a value of $10.00 per contract, a one-point move in gold will earn you $100 (not factoring in commissions and slippage). See the table below for other typical futures contracts specifications. (Margin requirements vary.)

Symbol	Contract	Exchange	Minimum fluctuation	Minimum fluctuation value	Full point value	Margin	Contract size
GC	Gold	COMEX	$0.10 per ounce	$10.00 per contract	$100	$4,125	100 troy ounces
CL	Crude Oil	NYMEX	1 cent per barrel	$0.01 per contract	$1,000	$4,675	1000 gallons
HO	ULSD NY Harbor	NYMEX	0.01 cent per gallon	$4.20 per contract	$42,000	$5,390	42,000 gallons
ZB	T-Bond	CBOT	32nds of a point	$31.25 per contract	$1,000	$3,740	$100,000
ZW	Wheat	CBOT	1/4 cent per bushel	$12.50 per contract	$50	$1,650	5,000 bushels
NQ	E-Mini Nasdaq 100	CME Globex	0.25 points	$5.00 per contact	$20	$3,960	$20 times Index
ES	E-Mini S&P 500	CME Globex	0.25 points	$12.50 per contract	$50	$5,060	$50 times Index

Table 1 - Sample Futures Contract Specifications

The futures markets appeal to me because they are available around the clock. They enable me to trade currencies like the Euro or Australian Dollar, energy commodities like heating oil or natural gas, and agricultural commodities including wheat or soybeans.

With futures, while one may argue that large players may manipulate a market (an illegal activity), there is no insider trading, as with a stock. Also, there is no CEO who can be charged or fired, drops in dividend don't affect contract values, and a future won't go out of business.

Forex

In the foreign exchange or forex markets, investors and traders attempt to earn profits through the varying values of pairs of currencies. The first forex trading platforms appeared in the late

1990s. Before this, forex trading was only available to very large traders and financial institutions. Since then, retail forex trading has become very popular, attracting many newcomers with its potential for easy profits and extremely high levels of leverage.

Currency fraud in forex markets between 2001 and 2007 resulted in $460 million of losses to retail traders. This prompted the US in 2010 to implement strict regulations to protect retail forex traders from currency swindles ... and from themselves. Previously, forex markets in the US had leverage caps set at 100:1. However, since 2010-11, new laws and oversight by the CFTC and the NFA exist to protect unwitting traders unable to manage high leverage levels. They now regulate forex markets in the US to 25:1 leverage level.

Some unregulated offshore brokers offer up to 2000:1 leverage. That's great if you know what you are doing, but such leverage can result in disaster for unprepared traders who risk extensive losses if a trade goes against them. Note also that in countries that have imposed regulation, the leverage maximums are still very high - as much as 200:1 in the UK and some other European countries.

A forex trader needs to remember that forex is a market that was designed originally for large sophisticated institutional traders with very deep pockets - not for the retail trader. Such large banking institutions can manage the swings in a highly leveraged market. The typical retail trader cannot.

Back in 2010, I was looking into forex market trading but was discouraged by the lack of regulation, the levels of fraud being reported, the excessive leverage and the risk of massive losses.

I still do not trade the forex markets because, unlike stocks or futures, there is no central exchange or central regulator. This absence makes me nervous. My decision is more a personal preference than anything else because I am used to trading on centrally regulated exchanges. However, I won't rule out pursuing forex markets at some point because of the leverage opportunities.

You can find a wealth of information on each of the asset classes on-line and in books, which provide useful starting points for your further investigation.

Things to Remember

- Each asset class has differing characteristics and tendencies
  – advantages and disadvantages.

- Leverage is to your advantage when not excessive and when managed accordingly.

- Stocks are limited to 2:1 leverage through the use of a margin loan.

- Futures markets are very diverse, with many choices of what to trade. In established centralized and regulated exchanges, there is attractive leverage up to 15:1 in US markets. Other markets may differ.

- Forex markets are currency focused, 'Over the Counter' (OTC) markets, many of them unregulated without oversight. Leverage varies from 25:1 maximum in the US to up 2000:1 in unregulated markets (in my view, excessive leverage for the average retail trader).

- Avoid trading forex with brokers with no regulation due to fraud risk and excessive leverage.

Chapter 8

Assessing a Trading System

Introduction

This is the first of four chapters that will make you aware of what you need to consider when assessing a trading system for trading markets either manually or automatically.

Anytime you are considering purchasing software, a training course, or a system in a book or an article, you should apply sound assessment criteria.

Obviously, this applies primarily to mechanical trading systems. However, since discretionary systems typically have mechanical aspects to them, if a detailed trade history is available, it could be analysed to broadly assess some aspects of the trading approach.

Equity curves, the number of trades and other performance parameters are built from the trading history and could then be evaluated. The intuitive, subjective aspects of the approach would be much more difficult (or even impossible) to evaluate and any analysis would have to be viewed in that light.

Typically in most cases, that sort of trade history is not available for discretionary trading approaches and the necessary analysis is not able to be done. That is one of the reasons why I do not recommend discretionary trading in the first place ... and, again, why I believe you will have a greater chance of success as a systems trader.

Asset Class

Many technical analysts believe that a system that works in forex markets can be applied to commodities and stocks with equal success. However, as mentioned previously, different asset classes have different characteristics. As such, it is atypical to find a trading system that performs well over all asset classes. If a vendor claims that their system can be applied to all three market classes, be very suspicious. For this to be true, it would have to be an extremely robust system.

Also within asset classes, there are market groups. For example, in the commodities asset class there is a market group of index products, energy products, agricultural products, interest rate products, etc. These market groups can be viewed as asset subclasses that also can have differing characteristics.

Bottom line: Find out for what asset class, market group or particular market the system has been developed.

If the vendor claims it works in any market in any asset class, be very wary and simply have them prove it by providing equity curve and performance statistics for each market in each asset class for you to analyse via the forthcoming criteria.

Probably, the system has been developed to apply to a particular group of markets, which is fine. Again have them provide proof. The more markets that the system works on, the more robust the system ... and the more markets you can apply the system to, which increases your opportunities to make more money.

In the past, I preferred that any trading system work on more than a single market as a demonstration of its robustness. However, experience has taught me that systems developed or tailored to work on a single market can be very desirable. Just be aware as you assess the system that you won't be able to scale it to other markets.

System premise

When assessing a trading strategy or system, you will need to know what the drivers are for the strategy. Is it 'mean reversion' or 'trending based'? Also, what is the edge?

What are the rules of the strategy? Whether you are considering a manually executed system or a fully automated closed (black box) system, you need to understand the rules that make up the system and the basis for the rules.

- Is it based on technical analysis, or fundamentals analysis premise, or a mix of the two?
- Does it enter trades based on a price pattern, moving average crossover, a pullback with higher time frame trend filter, increased volatility, the release of a fundamental report (i.e.: Weekly Natural Gas Storage Report or FOMC Report)?

There is an infinite number of premises and rules combinations that may drive and make up a trading strategy. Know what, and how many, are used in the system under consideration.

Lastly, does the system trade long or short trades or both? My preference is that a system has rules for entry for both long and short conditions. If it is designed to be a with-trend system, it should enter when the market is trending upwards as well as when down-trending. A well-designed system will have some symmetry between the number of long trades v. short trades and should not be one sided.
If it is one-sided, say 200 long trades, but only 50 short trades, more than likely it was not developed and tested properly.

Things to Remember

- Ask for which asset class, market group, or individual market the system has been developed. If the claim is that the system will work on all asset classes and markets, be extremely wary.

- Ask what are the rules for the strategy. The entry rules, the exit rules.

- The more rules there are, the less robust the strategy will be. (More detail in chapter 10.)

- Lean towards systems that enter trades both long and short, avoiding systems that are considerably biased towards either trade direction.

Chapter 9

Assessing the Equity Curve

Profitability over time

When evaluating a trading system, I look first at the equity curve graph. This graph represents the *historical* profit and loss of each trade cumulatively added together and plotted over the vertical axis as the equity range, and over the horizontal axis as the timespan (or trade number series) of the historical data.

Figure 4 below contains an example equity curve graph representing a single contract heating oil futures trading system.

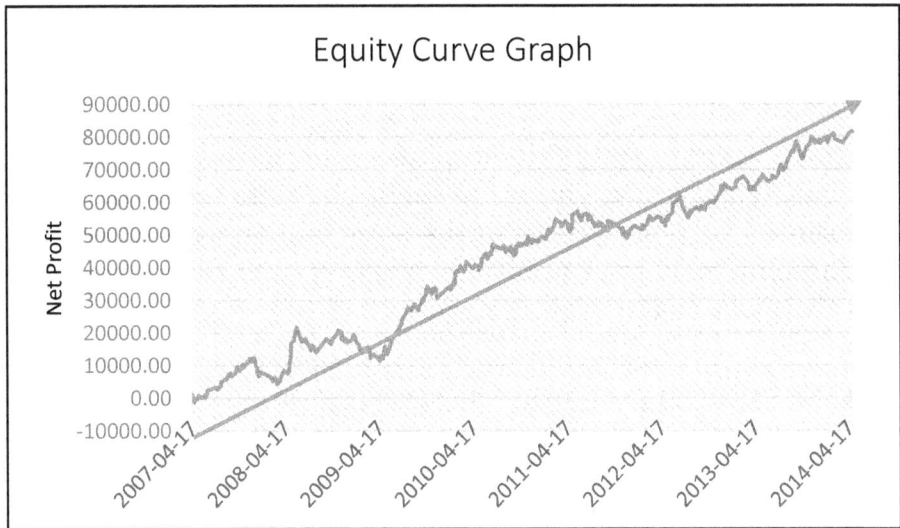

Figure 4 - Trading System Equity Curve Graph

This chart has a 45-degree diagonal line drawn upon it to represent a perfect equity curve with no drawdown. As perfection does not exist in trading, such equity curves do not exist in the real world.

If you are presented with such a perfect or near perfect equity curve, be suspicious of its pedigree as it is over-optimized or curve fitted (more on this later).

We can see that our equity curve tracks along the 45-degree equity line fairly well over the period. There are no long flat spots in the curve where it is not making money, which is good. You want to avoid any systems with equity curves that contain long timespans of sideways action. The curve should be marching steadily and profitably upwards, with the occasional retracement or drawdown periods.

Starting at the bottom left, we see that the account started with a balance of $10,000 and, over the time period of about seven years, ended up at the top left of the chart with a profit of around $80,000, averaging over $ 10,000 annually - a healthy amount for a single contract system.

Drawdown periods

Next let's take a look at the drawdown periods. These are key and, as you know from earlier chapters drawdown is represented by those points in the equity curve that move from a high point to a lower point when the system is losing money from the most recent high in profits.

In the chart below (Figure 5 – Equity Curve Drawdown Periods), the significant drawdown periods are labelled with circles A, B and C.

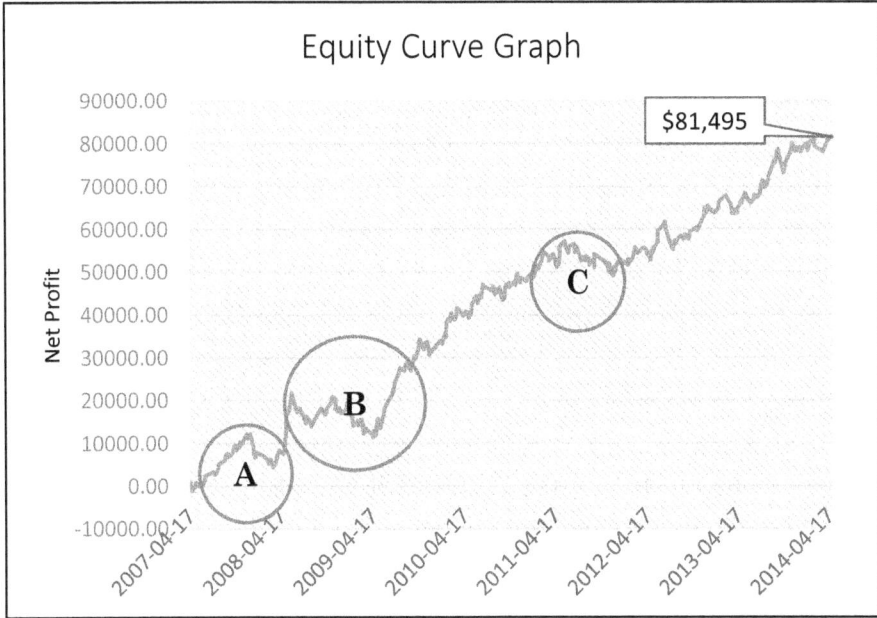

Figure 5 - Equity Curve Drawdown Periods

- Drawdown A has an equity high of approximately $12K and a low of $4K
- B has an equity high of about $21K with a low around $11K, and
- C has an equity high of about $57K with a low around $49K.

Looking at all three periods, the worst is B, with a $10K drawdown. That represents 12-13% of the total profits over the 7-year period of over $80K – an excellent drawdown ratio.

I look for drawdown to be between 10-20% of the equity total. Some traders can withstand more than that and, depending on the system, I may accept more - up to 30%. Some of the most profitable systems may have drawdowns of close to 70%, but the question is, can you live through a loss of close to 70% of your account?

Can you live with 50% or even 30%? I sometimes have a difficult time with 10% to 20%, but the fact is, you need to learn to live with drawdown if you want be successful in trading over the long run.

Imagine you have a $50K trading account and you are trading a system with 25% drawdown … meaning that you may start trading during a drawdown period and lose 12.5K or 25% of your account before you make any money.

The reality is you may lose a bit more than the historical drawdown in this circumstance before a profitable period begins. That's life as a trader. There is a reason for the disclaimers (*see Appendix I – The Usual Disclaimers*). Past performance does not guarantee future results, BUT if you are trading a system that is correctly developed and tested, you are maximizing the probabilities in your favour.

Keep imagining your $50K trading account. You have been trading our imagined system for a while, and your account balance is now at $39K. You've had 11 losing trades in a row. How do you feel? Are you going to stick with it and keep trading the system?

I can tell you that I have been in this situation many times. The single most important key to surviving drawdown is to maintain your belief in the system that you are trading. To maintain that belief, you need to know and understand how the system has been developed, how it has been tested and qualified. You'll need to be aware of and understand its key parameters and compare the current live trading performance to the historical performance. Over time and with experience you learn to manage yourself emotionally through these periods.

Now, let's get back to analysing the example equity curve above. We've noted that the average profit per year is more than $10,000; the maximum drawdown is 12% and that the shape of the curve is good v. the 45-degree equity line. What additional questions do we need to ask about it and the system?

Trade sources

We now need to know the source of the trades in the chart. That is, how the results represented in the equity chart were produced. This information is an important factor in determining the pedigree of the graph history and performance statistics.

There are two main types of trade sources, Live or real-time, and Hypothetical, which are broken down into distinct types: In-Sample and Out-of-Sample.

Live or real-time trades are actual trades that are executed in a live market environment with a broker and include slippage and commission. Live trades are the most desired trade history to obtain on any system. However an equity curve that contains ANY live trades, yet alone one comprising of 100% live trades is typically hard to come by. Many system vendors may not trade any of their available systems and do not have a live trading history available.

The bottom line is that you want to buy a system from a vendor that at least has some live trading history. Live trading results can be compared to the hypothetical trading results and confirm that the hypothetical trades in the equity curve represent what will occur in a live market environment.

With that confirmed, you will have a greater confidence in the hypothetical trading history performance characteristics.
Hypothetical trades are trades generated by the trading system software. They are a model of what was expected to occur

if the trading system was executing and trading with a broker in a live trading environment.

Note: I specify live trading environment because it is possible to trade a system with a broker in a simulated trading environment. In this case, the trading system is sending orders to the broker, but they are not sent to the actual market exchange for execution.

For our discussion, we will define two types of hypothetical trades:

a) Optimized (or in-sample)
Trading systems software, like any software application, is comprised of a series of inputs which are processed against a set of logic (or rules) and data, resulting in an output - in this case entry and exit signals.

Optimization is the process of finding the input parameter values that produce the best performance results over the test period. The system developer uses the in-sample period (ISP) to 'train' the system software on the market data under test.

b) Out of sample
Referring to Figure 6 below, trades that occur in the out of sample period (OSP) are simply traded in the period beyond the in-sample period where the system was trained or optimized.

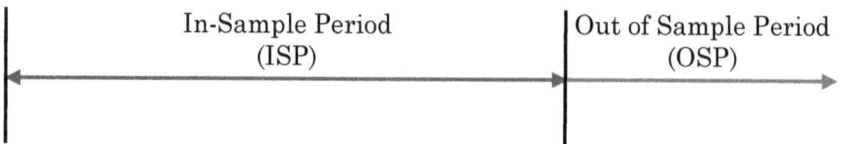

In-Sample Period (ISP)	Out of Sample Period (OSP)

Figure 6 - Sample Period – Out of Sample Period Timeline

System testing methodologies

The first system testing method [Figure 7] is an approach used by many inexperienced system traders, including myself when I first started out.

In-sample testing involves optimizing the system over the whole of the historical test period's data and evaluating the performance of the system based on that same optimized data set, then making the decision to trade the system live based on that performance evaluation.

Sadly, I can attest to the fact that this *does not work well.*

When applying this approach, my trading was inconsistent and resulted in a steadily decreasing trading account. Not fun. It worked so well in the historical test. What could be going wrong?

Optimization, at its best, is a training period that is correctly applied to the in-sample period with the expectation that the trading system will then be 'tuned' to the latest market data and will perform similarly in the 'out of sample' period, or live trading period. See in Figure 7 below.

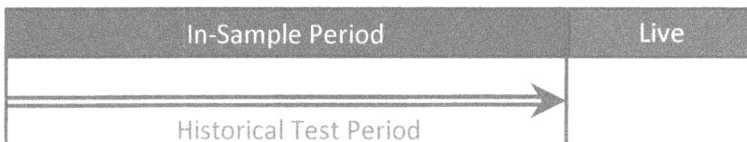

In-Sample Period	Live
Historical Test Period	

Figure 7 - In Sample Period Test Timeline

What was going wrong?

Optimization is easily and often abused by the inexperienced resulting in over-optimization or curve-fitting. Curve fitting is caused by so tightly tuning the inputs to the historical test data so that it will not work on new data. Contributors to curve fitting are the trading system having too many inputs and too many rules.

Furthermore, you typically don't know if you have over-optimized until you are running the system on unseen data, that is, live trading the out-of-sample period - a bit late if you wish to maintain your account balance above zero.

An example of an over-optimized system is seen in Figure 8 - Trading System Over-Optimization Example below.

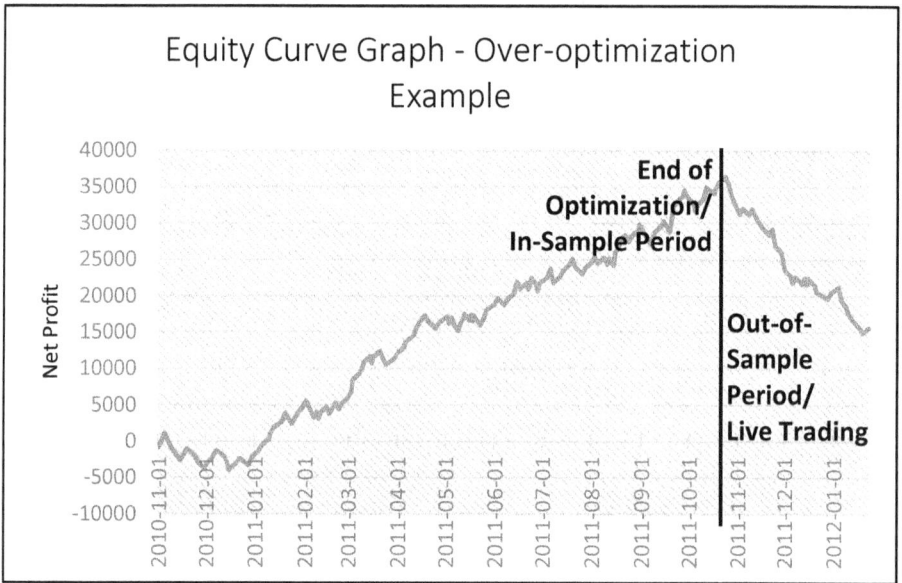

Figure 8 - Trading System Over-Optimization Example

The sad fact is that I (as any system developer/vendor) can make any system look like a peak performer during the optimization phase - as I did in the above example.

Again, I learned the hard way that system vendors might take advantage of this capability, advertising systems that look great on paper with excellent equity curves and performance statistics. BUT when the equity curve and performance statistics are based on the optimization or in-sample period, you have a high probability of getting similar results to the above example when you start to trade the system live ... resulting in you losing money and wondering why.

The next methodology involves performing the in-sample period optimization and testing the system on untested chart data - the out-of-sample period - to see how the system performs beyond the optimization phase and prior to trading live.

Although still hypothetical trades, they will give a level of confidence in the system that is not in the previous methodology. After a satisfactory performance in the out of sample period, the system is then traded live. (see Figure 9).

While the out-of-sample method is a marked improvement on the previous approach, its drawback is the optimized inputs are set as the best values for the system, with no opportunity to update them to changing market conditions.

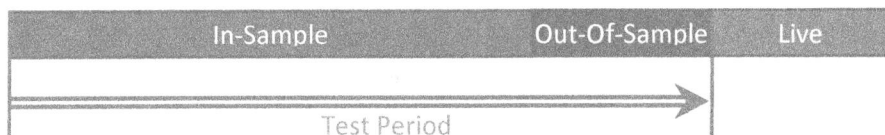

| In-Sample | Out-Of-Sample | Live |

Test Period

Figure 9 - In Sample Period – Out of Sample Period Test Timeline

Enter our third methodology. Walk Forward Analysis (WFA) solves that issue. As you can see in Figure 10, instead of a single ISP-OSP pair, multiple pairs are allocated to the test period. The WFA testing approach results in a more realistic testing of the system as markets change over time. Additionally, with multiple ISP-OSP pairs, the system inputs are optimized at intervals - which keeps the system tuned to the most recent market conditions.

This periodic tuning results in much more robust and reliable results than the previous two methodologies.

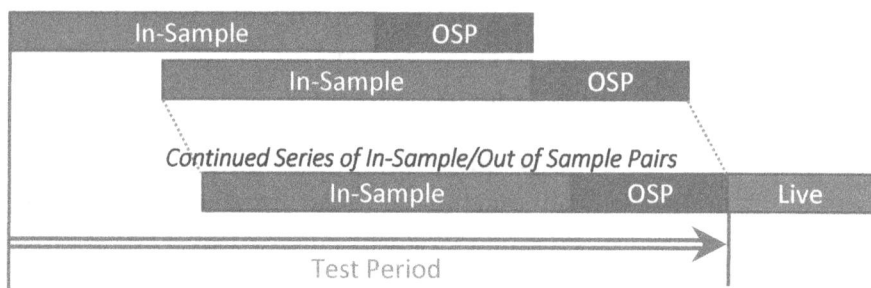

Figure 10 - Walk Forward Analysis Testing (In-Sample/Out-Of-Sample Pairs)

The obvious bottom line here is that, when evaluating a trading system, you want to select the system that has been historically tested using the WFA approach.

Your next step is to ask the vendor how many ISP-OSP pairs are contained in the WFA test period and how long the ISP and OSP periods are - which will be the same for all pairs. The length of the OSP will determine how often the system will need to be re-optimized, and will he/she provide the input parameter updates as part of the system's service or support, which should be included in the purchase.

In fact, the chart shown earlier (Figure 4 – Trading System Equity Curve Graph) is the equity curve of a sample WFA tested system. Covering an approximate seven-year WFA timespan, it contains 12 ISP-OSP pairs. The length of the ISP is 230 training days while the OSP is 130 trading days. So, the system requires updating about every six months.

Commissions and slippage

When evaluating an equity curve, it is crucial to ascertain whether or not commissions and slippage estimates are included. You need to know the amount of each and the basis for the slippage estimates.

Being fixed costs, commissions are simple. Brokers charge a fee for each trade that is executed, both on entry and on exit. The fee can be 'per trade' based, or based on per trade and number of contracts (or stocks) being traded.

For example, let's say I am trading one contract - the Australian Standard & Poor's 200 Index (SPI) future - and my broker charges $5.00 per trade. Then, each completed trade (entry/exit) cost me $10.00 in commissions. If I was trading two contracts, the total commissions charged would be $20.00.

Slippage is a more complex subject. It is the difference between the system's hypothetical or modelled trade entry and exit points versus what those points are in an actual live trading.

Slippage will vary, based on the type of orders that are employed by the system to enter and exit trades, and by the market and the bid/ask spread of the market at the time the order is executed at the broker.

Typically slippage will have a significant impact on the profitability of the system, and thus its equity curve.

For example, in Table 2 – Hypothetical v. Live Trade Results note the difference in the order generated by the trading simulation model against the actual filled trade execution entry and exits. You'll notice that the Live Profit & Loss (P/L) results show that the slippage figures used in the model (hypothetical trade) are very close to what occurs in a live trade, the live trading P/L with a more favourable result in some cases.

Symbol	Entry Date (ADT)	Exit Date (ADT)	Model Entry	Model Exit	Model P/L	FILLED Entry	FILLED Exit	LIVE P/L
HO #F	6/9/15 10:00	6/10/15 10:00	1.9048	1.9428	$1,511	1.9052	1.9427	1,577
HO #F	6/12/15 15:55	6/15/15 10:00	1.8871	1.8606	$1,028	1.8871	1.8590	1,178
HO #F	6/12/15 15:55	6/15/15 10:00	1.9362	1.9090	($1,227)	1.9365	1.9096	(1,130)

Table 2 - Hypothetical v. Live Trade Results

You can see the effect on the equity curve with and without slippage applied in Figure 11 – Slippage/No Slippage Equity Curves.

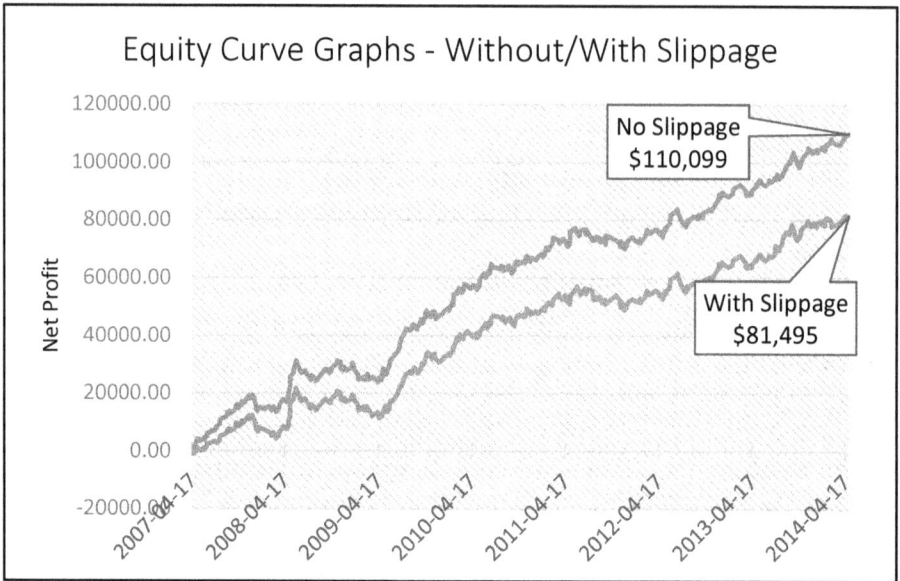

Figure 11 - Slippage/No Slippage Equity Curves

The change in total equity is apparent in the graph. Not visible is the positive effect of ignoring slippage will have on the performance statistics, like average trade, profit factor and others discussed in the next chapter.

I have encountered, and purchased systems from, vendors that do not include slippage in their marketing materials (equity curves/performance statistics).

So, when reviewing the equity curve graph you must confirm

- that the equity curve data include both slippage and commissions
- the basis of the slippage
- ascertain if the slippage is only an estimate or whether it has been verified by live trade history

- if an estimate, have the vendor justify the accuracy of the estimate.

Number of Trades

The total number of trades represented by the equity curve is important because you need to know if the number of trades is statistically significant and how often the system generates trades. Many trading books say that the number of trades must be greater than 30 to be statistically significant. (This based on minimum sample size as defined by statistical mathematics.)

I prefer to have a minimum history of 100 trades before I consider it. The point is to have enough trades over a long enough timespan to give you confidence that the system will work.

The timespan is important because you want the system to be tested over varying market conditions. Also, the number of trades per week, month or year must be considered from a personal preference standpoint. We will discuss personal preferences in 'Questions to ask yourself' in chapter 11.

The example system showed previously in Figure 4 – Trading System Equity Curve Graph has a total of 370 trades over a seven-year test period. It generates trades about once per week.

Just looking at the equity curve doesn't provide a rigorous, scientific method to assess a trading system, but it does provide an excellent vehicle for a preliminary analysis and a filter to reject undesirable systems. If the equity curve is not appealing, there is no need to look at the performance report.

Things to Remember

- Always assess the equity curve for angle, steadiness, profits per year, drawdown.

- Walk forward analysis is the accepted best method for historically testing systems and maximizing your probability of success.

- Insist on and confirm that slippage and commissions are included in any system being assessed. If they are not, walk away.

- It is best to have at least a sampling of live trade history to demonstrate the system in action and to confirm slippage estimates.

- Insist on a trading history of at least 30 trades, the more, the better. (Again, my preference is 100 or more).

Chapter 10

Assessing the Performance Report

At this point, you have evaluated the equity curve and concluded through your preliminary analysis that the system is worth looking into further.

The next step is to assess the performance report. System performance reports typically contain a somewhat daunting mix of calculated values, graphs of varying types and detailed trade listings. In my view, many of the parameters are not of much use - at least not to me.

Let's take a look at specific key parameters that I believe are most important and will enable you to evaluate a system confidently.

Data

The performance report should be based on either live data or, more typically, data from a walk-forward test, as noted in the previous section on system testing methodologies. My typical minimum historical testing timespan is five years. The more, the better. However this may vary depending on the number of trades and market conditions that occur over the test history.

The units being traded should be fixed i.e. with no position sizing applied.

- for futures-based systems, it should be trading a single contract,
- for a stock system, a fixed number of shares,
- for a forex currency, a single or fixed number of lots.

That's because position sizing can greatly enhance the performance of what may be a mediocre trading system. It is also much easier to compare performance reports if no position sizing is applied.

Key Report Parameters

Commissions paid and slippage paid totals will be contained in the performance report. If either of them is zero, move on.

Commissions (for futures single contracts) should be at least $5.00 'round turn', that is $2.50 per entry, $2.50 per exit on a single contract. (Some futures contracts may be more per entry and exit, but that is usually only when trading on non-US-based futures contracts and will depend on the broker).

In the example report, Figure 12, the commission paid is $1,719. The slippage paid is $29,640, which is quite substantial. However, this needs be viewed in the context of the entire system, and as a cost of doing business. Based on the performance report data, although the system paid $29K in slippage - which comes out of profits - it made $81K with a manageable drawdown. These are very reasonable trade-offs.

As discussed in the equity curve chapter, many factors contribute to slippage as it is a key element in system evaluation. Again, confirm the basis of the values and whether they have been validated with live trade history by the developer.

	All Trades	Long Trades	Short Trades
Net Profit	$81671.6	$33785.08	$47886.52
Gross Profit	$239949.84	$123172.76	$116777.08
Gross Loss	($158278.24)	($89387.68)	($68890.56)
Adjusted Net Profit	$52586.98	$12745.54	$27796.8
Adjusted Gross Profit	$223149.99	$111209.16	$104980.81
Adjusted Gross Loss	($170563.01)	($98463.62)	($77184.01)
Select Net Profit	$53196.28	$17319.64	$35876.64
Select Gross Profit	$178602.84	$91720.8	$86882.04
Select Gross Loss	($125406.56)	($74401.16)	($51005.4)
Account Size Required	$10335.32	$10339.24	$10792.56
Return on Account	790.22%	326.77%	443.7%
Return on Initial Capital	816.72%	337.85%	478.87%
Max Strategy Drawdown	($11767.52)	($11449.68)	($12162.4)
Max Strategy Drawdown (%)	(39.37%)	(47.28%)	(55.58%)
Max Close To Close Drawdown	($10335.32)	($10339.24)	($10792.56)
Max Close To Close Drawdown (%)	(35.48%)	(42.25%)	(52.4%)
Return on Max Strategy Drawdown	6.94	2.95	3.94
Profit Factor	1.52	1.38	1.7
Adjusted Profit Factor	1.31	1.13	1.36
Select Profit Factor	1.42	1.23	1.7
Max # Contracts Held	1	1	1
Slippage Paid	$29640	$16240	$13400
Commission Paid	$1719.12	$941.92	$777.2
Open Position P/L	($176.72)	n/a	($176.72)
Annual Rate of Return	115.79%	47.9%	67.89%
Monthly Rate of Return	9.65%	3.99%	5.66%
Buy Hold Return	$5853.62	$5664.23	$5853.62
Avg Monthly Return	$958.76		
Monthly Return StdDev	$2876.68		

Figure 12 - Sample System Performance Report - Page 1

Net profit is the overall profit or loss achieved by the trading system over the historical test period. *(If you have noticed that the figure 5 - equity curve graph profit is around $90K that is because it reflects a starting account size of $10,000.)* Net Profit is used to calculate Net Annual Profit, which is calculated by dividing the total net profit by the number of years of trade history.

As noted previously, I like this to be $10,000 or more. However, I would not eliminate systems around $7,500 if they have overall excellent performance and meet the minimum number of trades requirement. The example report confirms a net profit of $81,671 over a Trading Period of seven years, making a Net

Annual Profit of $11,660.

Maximum strategy drawdown is the greatest loss drawdown from the previous equity high, across all trades in the historical test period. Previously, this was discussed when looking at the equity curve graph, and the actual number can be confirmed in the performance report.

I look for the drawdown to be between 10-30% of the equity total. The example, with a Net Profit of $81,671 and a Maximum Strategy Drawdown of $11,767, puts the maximum drawdown to profit ratio at 14%. This is a bit more than our equity curve graph-based percentage of 12% and is perfectly acceptable.

Profit factor is calculated by dividing the gross profit (total of all profitable trades) by the gross loss (total of all losing trades), and represents the amount of dollars won for every dollar loss over the course of the trading history.

For a WFA developed and tested system, I like to see a profit factor of 1.5 and above, but I consider 1.3 perfectly acceptable, as you can still earn plenty of profits at that level. I would be wary of claims over 2.0, but, of course, the proof is in the trade history and, if that criterion is met as well as the others, you can have confidence in the system. Profit factor in the example report is 1.52, which is perfectly acceptable.

Total number of trades (see Figure 13) is a tally of all the entered and exited trades that occurred over the historical test period. I typically like to see in the neighbourhood of 100 trades, as this typically for me, represents a minimum significant enough number of trades to assess the system's performance. This is only a starting point, though, as the minimum required number of trades is better determined based on the number of inputs that make up the system.

The greater the number of rules or inputs, the greater the number of trades required. Look for 30 to 100 trades per rule. As an alternative, you can also apply this rule to inputs. In the example trading system, we have a total of 370 trades in the test period. This system has a total of seven inputs. Two are optimized while five are fixed values.

Also note the long and short trade totals. 203 long trades and 167 short, which shows that the system is not one sided.

Average trade is calculated by dividing the total net profit by the overall number of trades, which results in the average profit over each trade. Trading a single contract, the average trade should be over $50. The higher the value, the better, as it allows for any small performance drift or errors that may occur.

This, along with profit factor, are excellent tools to use when comparing different systems, as slippage and commissions are reflected in them (as in all the statistics we are evaluating). In the example report, the average trade is $210.73.

Largest losing trade is self-evident. Compare it with the average losing trade. I like to check the balance. If, like in the example, the average losing trade is $953 and the largest losing trade is $3,100, you want to know how many times the maximum occurred and where they were in the equity curve graph. Then you can tell how often to expect that for a variation from the average losing trade.

The key is to understand the factors behind the variation so that you are able to manage your trading psychology and not lose faith in the system when a large loss occurs.

	All Trades	Long Trades	Short Trades
Total # of Trades	370	203	167
Total # of Open Trades	1	0	1
Number Winning Trades	204	106	98
Number Losing Trades	166	97	69
Percent Profitable	55.14%	52.22%	58.68%
Avg Trade (win loss)	$220.73	$166.43	$286.75
Average Winning Trade	$1176.22	$1162.01	$1191.6
Average Losing Trade	($953.48)	($921.52)	($998.41)
Ratio Avg Win / Avg Loss	1.23	1.26	1.19
Largest Winning Trade	$3103.16	$2779.76	$3103.16
Largest Losing Trade	($3104.44)	($3024.64)	($3104.44)
Avg # Bars in Trades	5.4	6	4.7
Avg # Bars in Winning Trades	6	7	4.9
Avg # Bars in Losing Trades	4.7	4.9	4.3
Avg # Bars Between Trades	n/a	n/a	n/a
Avg # Bars Between Winning Trades	65.3	130.3	143.6
Avg # Bars Between Losing Trades	83	145.1	206.6

Trading Period	7 Yrs, 27 Dys, 4 Hrs
Time in the Market	8 Mths, 26 Dys, 21 Hrs, 5 Mins
Percent in the Market	10.36%
Longest flat period	1 Mth, 10 Dys
Max Run-up Date	5/9/2008 9:00:00 AM
Max Drawdown Date	6/20/2008 9:00:00 AM
Max Strategy Drawdown Date	4/17/2009 11:00:00 AM
Max Close To Close Drawdown Date	4/17/2009 12:00:00 PM

Figure 13 - Sample System Performance Report - Page 2

Percent profitable is the percentage of winning trades generated by the system over the historical test period. It is more of a psychological factor than anything else. Perfectly good systems, typically trend trading systems, may have percentages in the thirties. The question is, can you stick with trading the system when you are losing 70% of the time.

For the average person this is extremely difficult, which is why I like to stick to a system in the 40-plus percentile range … and more preferably over 50%, as in the example, which is 55%.

Account size required represents the maximum 'close to close' drawdown times, the number of contracts, plus the margin requirement. However, this is not the recommended or most reliable method to determine how much you need in your trading account to safely trade the example or any other system.

The account size required is best determined through Monte Carlo simulation, addressed in the next chapter.

Again, performance reports vary depending on the originating platform, and may contain hundreds of parameters. While there are others that are useful, I consider the ones addressed here to be key in the assessment of a system.

Things to Remember
• Request a full system performance report from the system vendor and take the time to review it in detail.
• Note any questions you may have and resolve them with the vendor before any purchase.
• Over time as you gain experience, you may identify additional criteria to use in your system assessments.
• If a performance report is not available, but there is a live trading history available, a performance report can be built from that data.

Chapter 11

Assessing Additional Criteria

Depending on the system development platform, 'expectancy' and Monte Carlo-related statistics may or may not be part of a systems performance report, but both are very useful. Monte Carlo analysis is mandatory in assessing any trading system. Keep in mind that all these parameters and statistics can be calculated from a trade history (Trade no., Entry price, Exit price, Date/Time, P&L).

Along the lines of 'trading a system that fits you', it is also important to ask yourself some questions and start to define your trading system preferences.

Expectancy

Expectancy represents how much the system will earn for every dollar that is risked. There are two methods of calculating expectancy, however, I prefer the calculation as defined by Dr. Van Tharp, a noted trading educator and doctor of psychology. For your reference, that calculation is

Expectancy = (Average Winning Trade X Percent Profitable
+ Average Losing Trade X 100
− Percent Profitable) ÷ (− Average Losing Trade)

I like expectancy to be 0.15 to 0.20 or more. Meaning that for every dollar I risk, I stand to earn 20 cents. In my view, anything lower than this figure would not be worth the effort trading.

Monte Carlo analysis

Monte Carlo methods solve many numerical and probability

questions in the scientific, financial and engineering fields. They use computer-based analysis of random experiments to create random scenarios or simulations. When applied to trading, the random experiments and scenarios are based on the system's trade history.

Even with a rigorous WFA-based development and testing methodology, there is uncertainty as to how the trading system will perform in the future on unknown data. Recall that 'prediction' is not a word that applies to trading and that most price action seen in a market is random data. Monte Carlo analysis can help to reduce that level of uncertainty - but not eliminate it.

The Monte Carlo simulation takes the trades in the historical test of the system, randomizes and rearranges the trade history, typically creating thousands of permutations of random scenarios of the trades. The scenarios are then analysed to identify the best and the worst performers, and assign confidence levels to the results.

This helps you assess how robust your strategy is, and what net profit and maximum drawdown you can expect from the system. Having better information supports your decision whether or not to trade the system, and reduces some of the uncertainty about its future performance.

I ran a Monte Carlo simulation for a one-year simulation period with 2,500 permutations, using our example systems trade history of 371 trades. See Table 3 – Sample System Monte Carlo Simulation (1 year) Results.

Start Equity	Risk of Ruin	Mean Drawdown	Mean Return	Return to Drawdown Ratio	Probability of Profit > 0
$15,000	4%	22.4%	93%	4.09	93%
$18,750	1%	19.5%	72%	3.63	95%
$22,500	0%	17.0%	60%	3.54	96%
$26,250	0%	15.1%	52%	3.35	94%

Table 3 - Sample System Monte Carlo Simulation (1 year) Results

In effect, my Monte Carlo simulation created 2,500 random scenarios, essentially 2,500 random equity curves, each depicting a hypothetical trade history over a one-year period. With 2,500 possible equity curves, you can generate data, which will help you to evaluate the system. They also model realistic scenarios for what could happen when trading the system live.

From our Monte Carlo simulation we have the following new statistics to evaluate on our system:

Start equity is the sum in the trading account when you start trading the system (after the end of the historical test period). So, if you were to decide to trade the system live, you would open your broker's account and fund it at this level.

Risk of ruin is the percentage chance or probability that the balance in your account will be below the minimum equity required. That is the point at which you typically must STOP trading the system, as it is now performing below its expected performance levels, as determined by the Monte Carlo simulation.

The stop trading point is an input into the Monte Carlo simulator. In our example, I have chosen a stop trading account level of $8,000. Therefore, in Table 3, if the account is funded at a start equity of $18,750, there is a 1% chance that the account will drop to the $8,000 level and you should stop trading the system. I typically target a risk of ruin of 1-4% or less and fund my account accordingly.

Mean drawdown represents the midpoint or 50% value of the maximum percentage decrease in the account size from an equity peak over the number of scenarios (2,500 in this case).

In the case of Table 3 row two, the mean maximum drawdown shows that, within a year over a distribution of 2,500 equity curve scenarios, the system has a 50% chance of reaching a drawdown of 19.5%. Like the maximum strategy drawdown addressed previously, I look for this to be 10-30%.

Mean return percentage is the closing equity minus the start equity over one year (divided by the start equity to convert it to a percentage) and is computed from a distribution of net profit of the 2,500 simulated equity curve scenarios over the one- year simulation period.

Return to drawdown ratio is the mean average percentage return divided by mean maximum percentage drawdown over the one-year simulation period. My preference is that this be at or above 2 - the higher above 2, the better.

Probability of profit > 0 represents the percentage probability that the system will be profitable over the first year. All of the rows in Table 3 have high percentages, indicating that the system should be profitable.

Monte Carlo analysis is not without its weaknesses, one being that it assumes the input trades from your trade history represent the only possible trades, and we know that we cannot predict the future. Anything can happen when you start to trade on live or unseen data. This analysis depends on the mean and standard deviation of the historical trades being accurate to produce meaningful results.
Other drawbacks exist, including autocorrelation, which relates

to trading systems where trade results depend on previous trades, but it does not apply in this case.

This has been a very brief and simple look at Monte Carlo analysis. When considering any system, you need only to verify that such an analysis has been completed and evaluate and understand the resultant statistics.

Questions to ask yourself

Many trading books state that you must find a system that fits your personality. While I generally agree with this, I must add the caveat that you may also have to adjust your personality because you may not find a successful system that syncs with your individual personality and expectations.

I'll present an example, but first let's look at Table 4 below which contains a by-no-means exhaustive list of some typical trading preferences. Take a look at each and make a note of five or six that resonate with you.

No.	Trading Preferences
1	I prefer to trade with statistically proven technical analysis methods only.
2	I prefer to trade with the trend (you define time frame).
3	I prefer to trade against the trend [Mean Reversion] (you define time frame).
4	I prefer to buy dips [With-Trend] (you define time frame).
5	I prefer to sell rallies [Mean Reversion] (you define time frame).
6	I prefer to hold positions as long as necessary (1 to 100 days).
7	I prefer to hold positions for a short time (1 to 5 days).
8	I prefer to trade intraday only, closing out all positions.
9	I prefer to trade a fixed number of shares or contracts.
10	I prefer to trade a variable number of shares or contracts.
11	I prefer to trade a small number of markets or stocks (1 to 5).
12	I prefer to trade a diversified portfolio (more than 10 stocks or markets).
13	I prefer to trade using cycles because I can anticipate changes.
14	I prefer to trade price patterns because I can react immediately.
15	I prefer to trade with price oscillators.
16	I prefer to read the opinions of others on the markets I trade.
17	I prefer to use only my own analysis of price action.
18	I prefer to use daily data in my analysis.
19	I prefer to use Intraday data in my analysis.
20	I prefer to use weekly data in my analysis.
21	I prefer to trade with an automated trading system.
22	I prefer to use discretion, matching wits with the market.
23	I prefer lots of fast action in my trading.
24	I prefer to trade with a trading system manually.
25	I prefer to use stop orders to control my risk.
26	I prefer to trade with variable-length moving average systems.

Table 4 – Core Trading Preferences List

These preferences can and will change over time. Over my journey, I have developed the following core beliefs listed in Table 5 – My Core Trading System Preferences.

No.	Trading Preferences
1	I prefer to trade with the trend in the 45 to 480 min timeframe.
2	I prefer to hold positions for a short time (1 to 10 days).
3	I prefer to trade a variable number of shares or contracts.
4	I prefer to trade a small number of markets: 1-10 (Futures).
5	I prefer to use stop orders to control my risk.
6	I prefer to trade with an automated trading system.

Table 5 - My Core Trading System Preferences

I tend to like to be in the market for as short a time as possible, which is one of the reasons I gravitated towards day-trading. Trading each day and getting out of the market at the end of the day made great sense to me. Being uncomfortable with the risk, I did not like holding trades overnight.

So, when I first started to trade automatic systems, I focused on day-trading systems with five-minute bars, since that is what I typically day-traded manually. One of my trading beliefs was number 8 in Table 4 because of what I then perceived as too much risk. I did not want to hold trades overnight.

I found through my own experience and talking to more experienced developers, that it is extremely difficult to design a day-trading system on short bar timeframes and be able to make money over the long haul.

When I say that I learned by experience, I mean that I learned the hard way. For example, I bought short bar day-trading systems offered by a CTA with over 20 years' experience. The optimized equity curves looked really great. However, my trading them live yielded very different results.

I have yet to find such an automated system that is properly tested and includes slippage and commissions in historical testing that meets my assessment criteria. (Not to say that I won't stop looking or that it doesn't exist.)

If you want success in trading, you may have to adjust your personality to fit the trading realities that exist. Over the years, that is what happened to me.

It is a good idea that you attempt to capture what your core trading preferences or expectations are. The difficulty or ease of this task is most probably dependent on your exposure to trading.

Put some serious thought into creating a list of *your* top 5 or 6 trading system preferences and record them. (The list can also be found in Appendix II – Example Core Trading System Preferences.)

You can refer to them when you are considering any trading system and update them as they change as your progress through your trading journey.

Resource: If you would like a free system performance assessment spreadsheet visit www.automatedonlinetrading.com, where you also will find helpful tools for Monte Carlo analysis, among others.

Things to Remember

- Monte Carlo risk analysis is a necessary pre-requisite to trading any system live.

- Use Monte Carlo risk analysis to determine minimum account funding requirements and the risk of ruin level of the system.

- Assess your trading personality and determine your preferences to use as a filter in selecting trading systems.

- If you want success in trading, you may have to adjust your personality to fit the trading realities that exist.

Chapter 12

The Long and Short of It

Earlier, we noted that, although over 90% of traders lose money, there are definite opportunities to MAKE money trading the financial markets.

We then explored the factors that contribute to failure in the markets due to industry misinformation and deception, which contributes to

- the use of unreliable technical analysis methods
- over-expectations of profit
- the learning curve required to become proficient.

We also discussed the many cognitive biases that can work against you as a trader ... as well as other factors including under-capitalization.

We then explored key factors that can contribute to success in the markets such as:

- Awareness of the two overall market forces that exist in every market
- Asset classes that have tendencies towards one or the other market forces - thus the two aligning trade categories (With-Trend or Mean Reversion)
- Trading with a proven edge in a market
- Trading with a properly developed and qualified system (WFA)

In previous chapters addressing how to assess trading system, I guided you through a process of evaluating a trading system or a trading approach – that is, any system for which the trade history is available. If no computer-based performance report is available, trades can be captured in a spreadsheet and processed to produce the statistics that were assessed.

In my view, you should not be trading using any method be it discretionary or systematic (manual or automatic) if you don't have the data on which to complete an informed evaluation of the proposed trading approach.

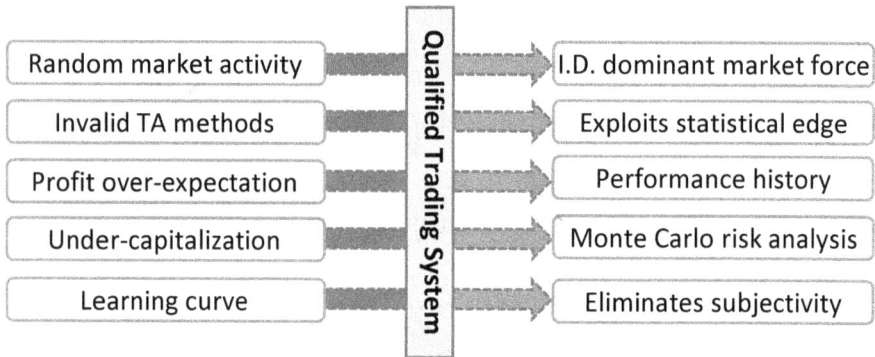

Figure 14 - Qualified Trading System Mitigation of Failure Factors

As you would now realise, I am an advocate of system trading. My key reasons (see Figure 14) are that in the process of developing a qualified trading system:

- random market gyrations are avoided, and the edge that is identified can be exploited for profits.
- the profits are then confirmed through back testing over historical data and by building a history of trades.
- equity curve and performance statistics are analysed to confirm the expected profits.
- historical trades are analysed with Monte Carlo methods to determine the system's proper capitalization.
- being a mechanical system, there is no need to interpret market movements - as a discretionary trader does by applying intuition based subjective methods, which decreases your learning curve and time.

While it could be said that system trading mitigates some of the cognitive biases because you have black and white entry and exit rules, it can still be difficult to have the discipline to stick with the system. Human factors like fatigue or sickness also can affect your performance.

Automation of the trading system is the next step.

Through automation of a trading system, cognitive biases can be further mitigated. That's mitigated, not eliminated. Overconfidence bias, confirmation bias, anchoring bias, hindsight bias, illusion of control and recency bias will still tug at you.

However, since the trading system software is making the decisions - and if you have the required level of trust in the system (which you will, as you have properly qualified it) - I believe that the impacts will be minimal.

Loss aversion or risk bias will still raise their ugly heads when you are in your ninth losing trade and $7,000 in drawdown. You may then be wondering whether to turn on the system today. However, you have the performance statistics telling you that a $7,000 drawdown has happened before, and the equity curve has recovered back into profits ... so hang in there and turn it on.

Further, trading errors due to you not feeling well or being tired or stressed can be mitigated almost to the point of elimination because it the software is making the decisions.

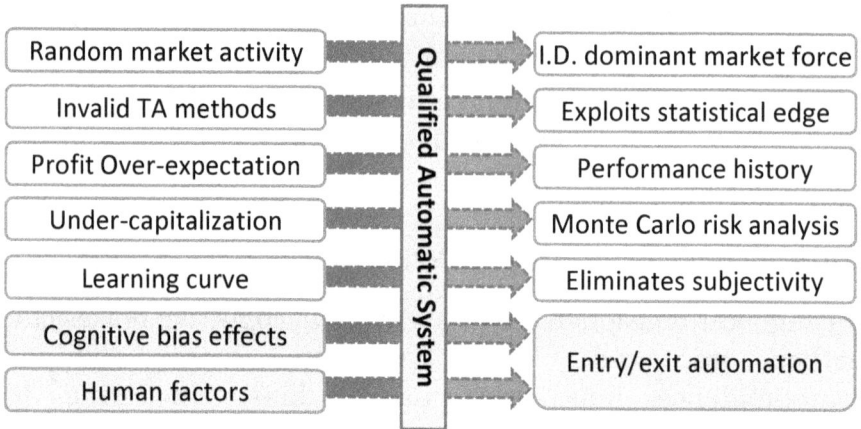

Figure 15 - Qualified Automatic Trading System Mitigation of Failure Factors

Figure 15 summarizes the key reasons why I am an *automated* system trader, why I develop my systems specifically for trading automatically and why I actively trade with them.

We'll now take a high level look at what is required to implement an automated trading system (see Figure 16 - Automated Trading Network Diagram.)

Automated trading systems use software code that executes on an automated trading platform installed on a computer. That computer can be located possibly at your home, or on a Virtual Private Server (VPS) that is connected via the Internet to a data feed and your broker. In turn, the broker is connected to the exchange that hosts the market you are trading.

Chart data from the Market Data Source is read by the automated trading platform hosted on your computer and monitored by the trading system software. When the entry criteria are met, the order is submitted automatically to your broker - then from your broker to the exchange to be filled. The trading software manages your trades throughout the trading process through to submitting the exit order and completion of the trade.

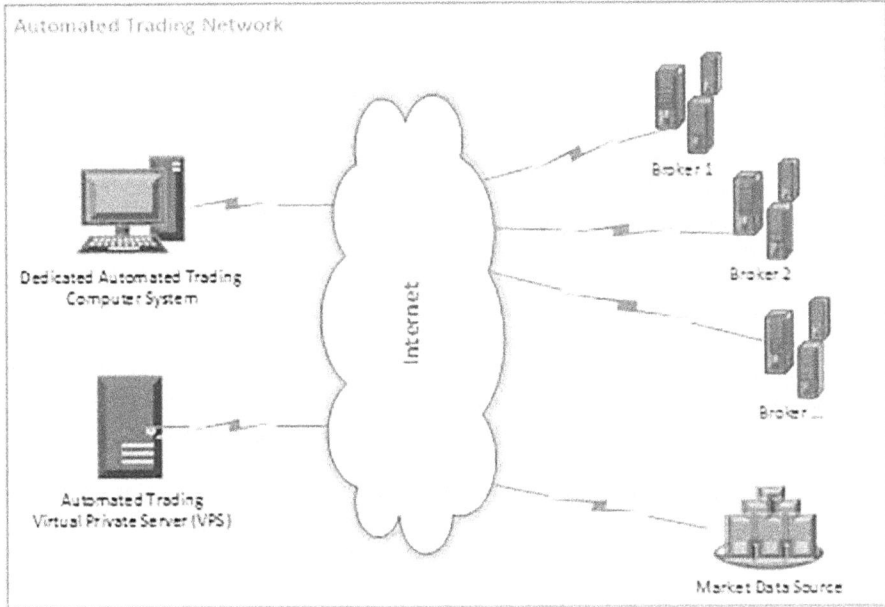

Figure 16 - Automated Trading Network Diagram

Automated trading platforms can trade multiple trading systems over multiple markets at the one time, managing and monitoring each of them.

Earlier we talked about the three 'E's - Education, Expertise and Experience. In my view, a properly developed and qualified *automated* trading system gives you immediate access to trading expertise as well as experience, all encapsulated in the system itself.

While you will have to learn how to manage your systems and get comfortable with the day-to-day monitoring and management process, a proper automated system can significantly shorten your journey to trading success.

Resource: For more information on automated systems trading visit www.automatedonlinetrading.com where you can learn details about setup, systems, and trading system development.

Things to Remember

- A properly developed automated trading system can mitigate many of the failure factors related to trading, increasing your probability of success.

- Automated trading systems fully automate trade entry and exit and are very reliable – when developed properly.

- Automated trading systems run on an automated trading platforms (MultiCharts, TradeStation, NinjaTrader ... several others), and are hosted on a computer either at your home or elsewhere on a server.

Chapter 13

A Final Test

Did you think you would be able to get away without a final test? Oh no, my friend, you are not so lucky. While finalizing this book, I received an interesting and all too common sales email. A snippet of the email is in Table 6 below. The complete email can be found in Appendix III – Test Materials.

Automate your trading with a one-of-a-kind strategy.
Performance Results from January 1, through July 10, 2015.
CL: $386,000.00 return, 89.08% winning trades, 3.57 profit factor.
ES: $177,015.00 return, 75.38% winning trades, 2.27 profit factor.
GC: $127,190.00 return, 86.33% winning trades, 2.69 profit factor.
TF: $197,690.00 return, 90.87% winning trades, 2.88 profit factor.
YM: $107,285.00 return, 90.34% winning trades, 3.28 profit factor.
The strategy works with Ninja Trader, Trade Station and Multi Charts.
To request a performance report on stocks, call or email us.
This strategy works on most tradable markets, including the ES, TF, GC, CL, YM, Stocks, and Forex.

Table 6 - System Advertisement Email Snippet

As you're reading it, based on what you have learned in this text, you should already hear alarms going off in your head.

Of course, I emailed the vendor and asked for an equity curve and performance report for the system, and the cost. He sent a report (no equity curve) for one of the markets, CL – Crude Oil, and also replied with the cost, US$2995. Excerpts from the report can be seen in Figure 17 below.

Here are your test questions:

1. Identify 3 key data points in the email that would cause you to doubt the veracity of the system being offered?

    a. _____

    b. _____

    c. _____

2. Review the performance report and identify at least 5 key parameters of the system. Evaluate each parameter and note why each would contribute towards a buying decision or a decision to reject the system?

    a. _____

    b. _____

    c. _____

    d. _____

    e. _____

3. State at least 3 additional questions you would propose to the vendor to assess the system.

a. _____

b. _____

c. _____

And that's it.

Resource: You can download a white paper with the answers to the test and other downloads at www.automatedonlinetrading.com\beatthemarkets

TradeStation Performance Summary			
	All Trades	Long Trades	Short Trades
Total Net Profit	$391,150.00	$200,200.00	$190,950.00
Profit Factor	3.58	3.84	3.35
Total Number of Trades	3486	1697	1789
Percent Profitable	89.10%	92.58%	85.80%
Avg. Trade Net Profit	$112.21	$117.97	$106.74
Largest Winning Trade	$600.00	$600.00	$600.00
Largest Losing Trade	($680.00)	($680.00)	($680.00)
Max. Consecutive Winning Trades	76	82	40
Max. Consecutive Losing Trades	3	4	4
Avg. Bars in Total Trades	5.28	5.57	5
Avg. Bars in Winning Trades	5.46	5.64	5.28
Avg. Bars in Losing Trades	4.83	4.71	4.93
Avg. Bars in Even Trades	1.33	7	1.28
Max. Shares/Contracts Held	4	4	4
Total Shares/Contracts Held	5808	2844	2964
Account Size Required	$2,460.00	$2,320.00	$2,720.00
Total Slippage	$0.00	$0.00	$0.00
Total Commission	$0.00	$0.00	$0.00
Trading Period	6 Mths, 4 Dys, 13 Hrs, 47 Mins		
Percent of Time in the Market	13.12%		
Time in the Market	24 Dys, 14 Hrs, 47 Mins		
Longest Flat Period	3 Dys, 19 Hrs, 21 Mins		
Max. Drawdown (Intra-day Peak to Valley)			
Value	($3,230.00)	($2,560.00)	($3,170.00)
Date	3/5/2015 10:28		
as % of Initial Capital	3.23%	2.56%	3.17%
Max. Drawdown (Trade Close to Trade Close)			
Value	($2,460.00)	($2,320.00)	($2,720.00)
Date	5/28/2015 8:00		
Max. Trade Drawdown	($680.00)	($680.00)	($680.00)

Figure 17 - Advertised Strategy Performance Report Excerpts

Chapter 14

Tapping My Knowledge

I sincerely hope that this book has been of value to you and has contributed to your understanding of the world of trading. That world is vast, and while there are many paths to success in trading, I truly believe that automated systems trading is the best choice for the well-informed retail trader.

To learn more about automated trading systems, please visit my website at *automatedonlinetrading.com*. I established Automated Online Trading (AOT) for the same reason I wrote this book; to help people take control of their investing and shorten their road to trading success with automated trading systems.

At AOT, we develop all of our systems applying rigorous system development, testing and qualification methods. This process sets AOT apart from other trading educators and system developers, and includes:

- trading idea development
- initial system feasibility testing
- in-depth optimization and testing
- complete walk-forward analysis
- unseen data trades history
- Monte Carlo risk analysis
- slippage and commissions included in all test phases
- position sizing analysis
- live trading simulation (with broker)
- live trading and monitoring

Many trading educators and system developers offer methods, strategies and systems (automated or manual) with insufficient performance data or historical proof that the approach actually works over the long term. They may teach a method that may not actually provide a proven edge in a particular market. All AOT offerings are fully automated and rigorously tested using the best methods available to the retail trader.

On the website you will find:

- further information on our development process
- performance details and weekly updates on our active systems
- new systems and their details as they become available
- video tutorials (under development) expanding on the book content, our development process, automated trading setup requirements, day-to-day monitoring and management

- discussion on various topics related to automated trading and trading
  in general
- trading tools – Monte Carlo Lab, Live Trading Daily Diary, Strategy Performance Spreadsheet (create performance report statistics based on manually input trade history) and more as available
- my list of recommended books and other trading information and
  product sources
- the opportunity to submit any questions, comments, suggestions you may have on the material in this book.

Our goal at AOT is to enable traders to be successful through down-to-earth education and rigorously developed and tested automated trading systems.

Thank you very much for reading this book. We look forward to your visit at *www.automatedonlinetrading.com* and wish you all the best in your trading.

References

Bhattacharya, S., & Kumar, K. (2006, 05 01). *A Computational Exploration of the Efficacy of Fibonacci Sequences in Technical Analysis and Trading.* Bond University, Faculty of Business Publications. Retrieved from http://epublications.bond.edu.au/: http://epublications.bond.edu.au/cgi/viewcontent.cgi?article=1032&context=business_pubs

Collins, A. (2006). *Beating the Financial Futures Market: Combining Small Biases into Powerful Money Making Strategies.* Hoboken: John Wiley & Sons, Inc.

Davey, K. J. (2014). *Building Winning Algorithmic Trading Systems.* Hoboken: John Wiley & Sons.

Grimes, A. (2012). *The Art and Science of Technical Analysis.* Hoboken, New Jersey: John Wiley & Sons, Inc.

Gupta, N. (2011, 01 01). *Fibonacci Retracements and Self-Fulfilling Prophecy.* Retrieved from http://digitalcommons.macalester.edu/: http://digitalcommons.macalester.edu/cgi/viewcontent.cgi?article=1041&context=economics_honors_projects

Malkiel, B. (2007). *A Random Walk Down Wall Street.* New York: W.W. Norton & Company Inc.

Taleb, N. N. (2004). *Fooled by Randomness - The Hidden Role of Chance in Life and in the Markets.* New York: Random House Publishing Group.

Tharp, D. V. (2007). *Trade Your Way to Financial Freedom.* New York, NY: McGraw-Hill.

Tushar S. Chande, P. (2001). *Beyond Technical Analysis - How to Develop and Implement a Winning Trading System.* John Wiley & Sons, Inc.

Appendix I The Usual Disclaimers

Below are typical disclaimers you should find in the fine print of any trading education providers guarantees, education material or legal notices and disclaimers web page, as you found in the front material of this book.

When I began trading, I would see these disclaimers and read them, but they did not sink in. It is very important that you take the time to read and re-read them to fully understand the details prior to any purchase of trading materials.

This one is my favourite as it, in my view, sums things up:

"The past performance of any trading system or methodology is not necessarily indicative of future results."

Knowing the randomness of markets and all the factors that can work against you as a trader, you can now understand why these disclaimers are legally required.

Below you will find three further examples of typical disclaimers.

Trading Education Provider Disclaimer

The information presented to you in our products is presented through use of examples only, do not constitute any securities recommendations and may or may not be suitable to any individual investor's needs.

We are not aware of your individual financial situation and make no recommendations as to the specific markets that you should trade or to the capital requirements for trading in any particular market or security.

While information provided in the products is drawn from sources considered reliable, we, the Author and their directors, officers, employees and consultants:

1) do not warrant or guarantee, expressly or impliedly that such information is accurate or current and

2) may, at any time, own or have agreed to buy or sell any securities presented in the products. The information used in the products is general investment education and neither constitutes, nor is intended to take the place of individual tailored advice from a professional investment advisor.

Before making an investment decision on the basis of the information used in our products, you need to consider, with or without the assistance of a licensed securities advisor, whether the advice is appropriate in light of your particular investment needs, objectives and financial circumstances.

U.S. Government Required Disclaimer

Commodity Futures Trading Commission (CFTC)

- Futures and Options trading has large potential rewards, but also large potential risk.

- You must be aware of the risks and be willing to accept them in order to invest in the futures and options markets.

- Don't trade with money you can't afford to lose.

- This is neither a solicitation nor an offer to Buy/Sell futures, stocks or options on the same.

- No representation is being made that any account will or is likely to achieve profits or losses similar to those discussed in this document.

- The past performance of any trading system or methodology is not necessarily indicative of future results.

Commodity Futures Trading Commission (CFTC) rule 4.41

Hypothetical or simulated performance results have certain limitations.

- Unlike an actual performance record, simulated results do not represent actual trading.

- Also, since the trades have not been executed, the results may have under-or-over compensated for the impact, if any, of certain market factors, such as lack of liquidity.

- Simulated trading programs in general are also subject to the fact that they are designed with the benefit of hindsight.

- No representation is being made that any account will or is likely to achieve profit or losses similar to those shown.

Appendix II Example Core Trading System Preferences

No.	Trading Preferences
1	I prefer to trade with statistically proven technical analysis methods only.
2	I prefer to trade with the trend (you define time frame).
3	I prefer to trade against the trend [Mean Reversion] (you define time frame).
4	I prefer to buy dips [With-Trend] (you define time frame).
5	I prefer to sell rallies [Mean Reversion] (you define time frame).
6	I prefer to hold positions as long as necessary (1 to 100 days).
7	I prefer to hold positions for a short time (1 to 5 days).
8	I prefer to trade intraday only, closing out all positions.
9	I prefer to trade a fixed number of shares or contracts.
10	I prefer to trade a variable number of shares or contracts.
11	I prefer to trade a small number of markets or stocks (1 to 5).
12	I prefer to trade a diversified portfolio (more than 10 stocks or markets).
13	I prefer to trade using cycles because I can anticipate changes.
14	I prefer to trade price patterns because I can react immediately.
15	I prefer to trade with price oscillators.
16	I prefer to read the opinions of others on the markets I trade.
17	I prefer to use only my own analysis of price action.
18	I prefer to use daily data in my analysis.
19	I prefer to use intraday data in my analysis.
20	I prefer to use weekly data in my analysis.
21	I prefer to trade with an automated trading system.
22	I prefer to use discretion, matching wits with the market.
23	I prefer lots of fast action in my trading.
24	I prefer to trade with a trading system manually.
25	I prefer to use stop orders to control my risk.
26	I prefer to trade with variable-length moving average systems.

Table 7 - Example Core Trading System Preferences

Appendix III Test Materials

System Vendor Email Advertisement

Automate your trading with a one-of-a-kind strategy.
Performance Results from January 1, through July 10, 2015.

CL: $386,000.00 return, 89.08% winning trades, 3.57 profit factor.
ES: $177,015.00 return, 75.38% winning trades, 2.27 profit factor.
GC: $127,190.00 return, 86.33% winning trades, 2.69 profit factor.
TF: $197,690.00 return, 90.87% winning trades, 2.88 profit factor.
YM: $107,285.00 return, 90.34% winning trades, 3.28 profit factor.

The strategy works with Ninja Trader, Trade Station and Multi Charts.

To request a performance report on stocks, call or email us.

This strategy works on most tradable markets, including the ES, TF, GC, CL, YM, Stocks, and Forex.

Whatever your preference: Swing, Position, or Day Trading, this strategy has performed nicely.

At this time we are offering for purchase a limited number of our Trading Strategies. The strategy can be purchased at this time, and implemented into your trading method right away; however, we are only selling a limited number. Therefore, if you are interested do not hesitate to give us a call and we will gladly discuss any questions you may have.

The Strategy is not sold on our website or advertised to the general public.
For more information or to order it call me at 775-443-7677 or email me at Xxxxx@xxxxxxxxx.com

All the CFTC, NFA, and SEC Disclaimers apply. More information about the Disclaimers can be found on our web site.
Thanks for doing business with us.

Sincerely,

Xxx Xxxxx
www.xxxxxxxx.com
XXX-XXX-XXXX

Table 8 - System Vendor Email Advertisement

Trading System Performance Report – Part I

TradeStation Performance Summary				
	All Trades	**Long Trades**		**Short Trades**
Total Net Profit	**$391,150.00**	$200,200.00		$190,950.00
Gross Profit	$542,990.00	$270,720.00		$272,270.00
Gross Loss	($151,840.00)	($70,520.00)		($81,320.00)
Profit Factor	**3.58**	3.84		3.35
Roll Over Credit	$0.00	$0.00		$0.00
Open Position P/L	$0.00	$0.00		$0.00
Select Total Net Profit	$389,950.00	$199,600.00		$190,350.00
Select Gross Profit	$541,790.00	$270,120.00		$271,670.00
Select Gross Loss	($151,840.00)	($70,520.00)		($81,320.00)
Select Profit Factor	3.57	3.83		3.34
Adjusted Total Net Profit	$372,097.13	$187,062.32		$177,152.25
Adjusted Gross Profit	$533,247.04	$263,889.82		$265,320.63
Adjusted Gross Loss	($161,149.91)	($76,827.50)		($88,168.38)
Adjusted Profit Factor	3.31	3.43		3.01
Total Number of Trades	3486	1697		1789
Percent Profitable	**89.10%**	92.58%		85.80%
Winning Trades	3106	1571		1535
Losing Trades	266	125		141
Even Trades	114	1		113
Avg. Trade Net Profit	**$112.21**	$117.97		$106.74
Avg. Winning Trade	$174.82	$172.32		$177.37
Avg. Losing Trade	($570.83)	($564.16)		($576.74)
Ratio Avg. Win:Avg. Loss	0.31	0.31		0.31
Largest Winning Trade	**$600.00**	$600.00		$600.00
Largest Losing Trade	**($680.00)**	($680.00)		($680.00)
Largest Winner as % of Gross Profit	0.11%	0.22%		0.22%
Largest Loser as % of Gross Loss	0.45%	0.96%		0.84%
Net Profit as % of Largest Loss	57522.06%	29441.18%		28080.88%
Select Net Profit as % of Largest Loss	57345.59%	29352.94%		27992.65%
Adjusted Net Profit as % of Largest Loss	54720.17%	27509.16%		26051.80%
Max. Consecutive Winning Trades	76	82		40
Max. Consecutive Losing Trades	3	4		4
Avg. Bars in Total Trades	5.28	5.57		5
Avg. Bars in Winning Trades	5.46	5.64		5.28
Avg. Bars in Losing Trades	4.83	4.71		4.93
Avg. Bars in Even Trades	1.33	7		1.28
Max. Shares/Contracts Held	4	4		4
Total Shares/Contracts Held	5808	2844		2964
Account Size Required	**$2,460.00**	$2,320.00		$2,720.00
Total Slippage	**$0.00**	$0.00		$0.00
Total Commission	**$0.00**	$0.00		$0.00

Figure 18 - Advertised Trading System Performance Report - Part 1

Trading System Performance Report – Part 2

Return on Initial Capital	391.15%		
Annual Rate of Return	309.92%		
Buy & Hold Return	-2.16%		
Return on Account	15900.41%		
Avg. Monthly Return	$55,878.57		
Std. Deviation of Monthly Return	$27,677.99		
Return Retracement Ratio	11.48		
RINA Index	49016.83		
Sharpe Ratio	n/a		
K-Ratio	n/a		
Trading Period	**6 Mths, 4 Dys, 13 Hrs, 47 Mins**		
Percent of Time in the Market	13.12%		
Time in the Market	24 Dys, 14 Hrs, 47 Mins		
Longest Flat Period	3 Dys, 19 Hrs, 21 Mins		
Max. Equity Run-up	$392,760.00		
Date of Max. Equity Run-up	7/14/2015 11:26		
Max. Equity Run-up as % of Initial Capital	392.76%		
Max. Drawdown (Intra-day Peak to Valley)			
Value	($3,230.00)	($2,560.00)	($3,170.00)
Date	3/5/2015 10:28		
as % of Initial Capital	3.23%	2.56%	3.17%
Net Profit as % of Drawdown	12109.91%	7820.31%	6023.66%
Select Net Profit as % of Drawdown	12072.76%	7796.88%	6004.73%
Adjusted Net Profit as % of Drawdown	11520.03%	7307.12%	5588.40%
Max. Drawdown (Trade Close to Trade Close)			
Value	($2,460.00)	($2,320.00)	($2,720.00)
Date	5/28/2015 8:00		
as % of Initial Capital	2.46%	2.32%	2.72%
Net Profit as % of Drawdown	15900.41%	8629.31%	7020.22%
Select Net Profit as % of Drawdown	15851.63%	8603.45%	6998.16%
Adjusted Net Profit as % of Drawdown	15125.90%	8063.03%	6512.95%
Max. Trade Drawdown	($680.00)	($680.00)	($680.00)

Figure 19 - Advertised Trading System Performance Report - Part 2

Acknowledgements

I wish to personally thank the following people for their contributions to my inspiration and knowledge and other help in creating this book:

Kevin Davey - Mentorship

Aik Peng Tan – Inspiration

Jared Danaraj - Support

Harold Abrahams – Editing and Copywriting

Angie at PRO_EBOOKCOVERS – Cover Design

Index

Stay Connected

Thank you for reading Beat the Markets!

Please stay connected via our website at www.automatedonlinetrading.com and social media via www.facebook.com/aotinternational.